Flying FOR HER COUNTRY

THE AMERICAN AND SOVIET WOMEN MILITARY PILOTS OF WORLD WAR II

AMY GOODPASTER STREBE

Foreword by Trish Beckman

Potomac Books, Inc.
Washington, D.C.

This paperback edition published in the United States by Potomac Books, Inc.

Flying for Her Country: The American and Soviet Women Military Pilots of World War II, by Amy Goodpaster Strebe, was originally published in hardcover by Praeger Publishers, http://www.greenwood.com/praeger, an imprint of Greenwood Publishing Group, Inc., Westport, CT. Copyright © 2007 by Amy Goodpaster Strebe. This paperback edition by arrangement with Greenwood Publishing Group, Inc. All rights reserved.

Library of Congress Cataloging-in-Publication Data
Strebe, Amy Goodpaster, 1969–
  Flying for her country : the American and Soviet women military pilots of World War II / Amy Goodpaster Strebe. — 1st ed.
    p. cm.
  Originally published; Westport, Conn. : Praeger Security International, 2007.
  ISBN 978-1-59797-266-6 (pbk. : alk. paper)
  1. World War, 1939–1945—Aerial operations, American. 2. World War, 1939–1945—Aerial operations, Soviet. 3. World War, 1939–1945—Participation, Female. 4. Women Airforce Service Pilots (U.S.)—Biography. 5. Women air pilots—United States—Biography. 6. Women air pilots—Soviet Union—Biography. 7. Air pilots, Military—United States—Biography. 8. Air pilots, Military—Soviet Union—Biography. I. Title.
  D790.S9435 2008
  940.54'49730922—dc22

                                                      2008027861

Printed in the United States of America on acid-free paper that meets the American National Standards Institute Z39-48 Standard.

Potomac Books, Inc.
22841 Quicksilver Drive
Dulles, Virginia 20166

First Edition

10 9 8 7 6 5 4 3 2

Flying FOR HER COUNTRY

THE AMERICAN AND SOVIET WOMEN MILITARY PILOTS OF WORLD WAR II

NATIONAL

WASP·WWII
MUSEUM

www.waspmuseum.org

Also by Amy Goodpaster Strebe

Desert Dogs: The Marines of Operation Iraqi Freedom

Similar Titles from Potomac Books

Before Amelia: Women Pilots in the Early Days of Aviation
Eileen F. Lebow

Women Warriors: A History
David E. Jones

Fruits of Victory: The Woman's Land Army of America in the Great War
Elaine F. Weiss

To Mom—For always believing in me

CONTENTS

Foreword by Trish Beckman ix

Acknowledgments xv

Abbreviations xvii

Introduction 1

1. America's First Women Military Pilots 4

2. Marina Raskova and Her Soviet Aviation Program 15

3. Patriotism and a Love of Flying 29

4. Gender Issues 37

5. The Ties that Bind 51

6. The WASP Are Disbanded 59

7. Demobilization of the Soviet Airwomen 70

Conclusion 75

Notes 85

Bibiliography 97

Index 105

FOREWORD

As a young girl growing up in Huntsville, Alabama, I was influenced by the space program and interested in all things mechanical: repairing automobiles, building model rockets, and flying radio-controlled airplanes. I loved math and science. During my twenty-eight years of active duty in the U.S. Navy, I earned a bachelor's degree and a master's degree in aeronautical engineering, completed flight training as a Naval Flight Officer, graduated from U.S. Naval Test Pilot School (and later instructed there), and was lucky enough to fly in sixty-seven types of military aircraft. The job I enjoyed the most was when I was responsible for the production of F/A-18C/D aircraft in St. Louis. It was very satisfying to fly as a Weapons Systems Operator in the F/A-18D, and to use my engineering skills to research issues related to the production process. It was also rewarding to see all the aircraft, for which I had responsibility during production, return home safely from the armed conflict known as Operation Desert Storm.

If it weren't for the women who went before me, in the civilian equal rights movement and in military aviation, I would not have had such rewarding professional opportunities. Even so, during most of my military career, men who were less qualified than I (in education, physical ability, and experience) were allowed access to aircraft that were denied to me. By law, those who genetically possessed the tiny y-chromosome were given precedence when aircraft assignments were made; men were presumed to have the exclusive right to fly combat aircraft.

When my Navy career began in 1970, I encountered some negative attitudes toward women in military aviation. Almost thirty years had passed since

American women had flown military aircraft, long enough for the men involved to conveniently "forget" the contributions made by women aviators in World War II. Only three years after the war ended, Congress enacted Combat Exclusion Laws that legalized the discrimination against women aviators.

My generation had to prove we could fly all over again. Fortunately, we had women role models and mentors to help us do this. The women who were my role models in the 1970s—and who became my mentors in the 1980s and later, when I was lucky enough to finally meet them—were the Soviet airwomen, the WASP (Women Airforce Service Pilots), and the female Navy navigators of World War II.

During the 1970s, race and gender rights were hotly debated. I remember one discussion with a young sailor who arrogantly asked me, "If women are as good as men, then why are there no famous women chefs?" I was taken aback by that question; "famous chefs" was not my area of interest or expertise (I had not yet heard of Julia Child); what did that have to do with the military, and how could he not know that "denied opportunity" might be the cause?

I believe the sailor intentionally picked that question in order to imply that "chef" was a career where only men were worthy, and that women (who do most of the cooking on the planet) were not capable of being "chefs" on par with men because men were superior in every possible way. But, if he had said that women were not capable of being military aviators I would have known exactly what to say: "You are wrong, wrong, wrong! Let me introduce you to the women who flew during World War II."

Before they were "officially" allowed to serve, women disguised themselves as men and served with the U.S. military beginning as early as the American Revolutionary War. The first women to serve officially in the U.S. armed forces were in the Army Nurse Corps beginning in 1901, and in the Navy Nurse Corps in 1908. In 1917, the U.S. Navy was the first military service to enlist women in fields other than as nurses; women also served proudly in the Marine Corps and the Coast Guard.

In 1915, following the sinking of the British hospital ship *Anglia*, the newspaper headlines called for the right to vote for heroines as well as heroes. The debate at the time was whether "the vote" was a reward for women's wartime loyalty. British women over the age of thirty were given the right to vote in 1918, and all women in Britain over the age of twenty-one gained suffrage in 1928.

Similarly in America, women's service during World War I was part of the debate in Congress, which in 1919 approved the Nineteenth Amendment (women's right to vote). American women had proved they were willing to serve in the military (Navy, Marine Corps, and Coast Guard), even before they could vote. The Amendment became law in 1920 following ratification by the States.

Some women seem to forget whose shoulders they walk on, ignoring the sacrifices of the pioneers who paved the road ahead of them. I often wonder how many American women, on their way to the polls to vote, know that many suffragists were imprisoned and some died in the struggle that eventually gave American women the right to vote in 1920. I also wonder how many American women appreciate the fact that military women, willing to defend our nation before they could even vote, helped women in the United States gain the right to vote.

In World War II, over 400,000 women served in all branches of the U.S. military. Women proved they could not only fly every type of fighter and bomber aircraft as the male pilots, but they could also build and repair the airplanes, among many other nontraditional jobs.

Until and throughout World War II, women were only welcome in the military during wartime when the threat of danger was more imminent. Ironically, it was in peacetime when men vocally professed their belief that women should be "protected and kept out of harm's way." In my opinion, what they really meant to say was that men needed to be "protected from equal competition with women" during peacetime.

It should come as no surprise that, as a compromise for allowing women to serve in the U.S. military during peacetime, Congress passed the Combat Exclusion Laws in 1948 to prevent women from serving in "aircraft engaged in combat missions" in the U.S. Navy and U.S. Air Force. Navy women were also prohibited from serving on combat ships. There has never been, however, a law restricting the assignment of Army women; only by policy have there been restrictions.

Following World War II, the number and types of jobs for servicewomen quickly dwindled. When I enlisted in the Navy in 1970, I was not permitted to be an aircraft mechanic or aviation technician (jobs that were previously held by Navy women in the war). As the Vietnam conflict ended in 1970, the U.S. military embraced the concept of an All-Volunteer Force (the men's draft ended), and women became integrated into the military services. More jobs were opened permanently to women, including the opportunities to train as military pilots (Navy in 1973, Army in 1974, Air Force in 1976).

Women were still limited to noncombat aviation roles, which only hindered their promotion potential but did not keep them out of harm's way. American women served in Panama, Grenada, and Desert Storm. They could be targets, but they were not allowed to shoot back. Yet they continued to serve faithfully.

During Operation Desert Storm the American people recognized the dedication of military women aviators, and in 1991 both houses of Congress voted to repeal the Combat Exclusion Laws. The policy finally changed in 1993 under the Clinton administration. Since then, American military women have flown aircraft engaged in combat missions, being allowed to shoot back—as Sabiha Gökçen did in Turkey in 1937 and Marina Raskova's three Soviet women's aviation regiments did in World War II.

As a military volunteer, I know why I was motivated to serve my country. While I cannot be sure what motivates other women and men to serve in the armed forces, I believe that Ralph Waldo Emerson expressed it well in his poem "Voluntaries" over 140 years ago:

> . . . In an age of fops and toys,
> Wanting wisdom, void of right,
> Who shall nerve heroic boys
> To hazard all in Freedom's fight . . .
>
> . . . So nigh is grandeur to our dust,
> So near is God to man,
> When Duty whispers low, Thou must,
> The young replies, I can . . .

It is unlikely that Emerson envisioned that "heroic boys" could someday be replaced by "heroic girls" willing to risk their lives in "Freedom's fight." Let us give Mr. Emerson the benefit of the doubt and assume he did not have access to any documentation suggesting that women, often disguised as men, had risked their lives in armed conflicts by the mid-1860s. But whether such documentation was missed, or dismissed, women had in fact served in combat.

By the beginning of the 1940s, women no longer had to disguise themselves as men to serve in combat. Hundreds of thousands of Soviet women took up arms in a variety of combat roles during the Great Patriotic War, including aviation. Some Soviet women flyers were so effective and feared that they were nicknamed "Night Witches" by their German foes.

American women aviators did not get the opportunity to serve in combat in World War II. Navy women, however, instructed men in the science of navigation, both on the ground and in the air. The WASP were civilians who flew ferrying missions and performed every duty inside the cockpit as their male counterparts aside from combat. It was not until 1979—thirty-four years after the end of the war—that the WASP achieved their long overdue, retroactive military veteran status. Had American women faced the same threat to U.S. soil as Soviet women faced in their own country during World War II, they would have served in combat willingly, I have no doubt. The women pilots' love of country and their love of flying were their passions—passions that we younger American military women have proudly inherited.

While several books have been written about the Soviet airwomen and the WASP, this is the first scholarly endeavor to weave together the women's wartime efforts within their historical context, while also boldly examining the gender roles of women during this period. Meticulously researched with the women veterans' own words as witness, this exceptional book pays tribute to the invaluable contributions made by the American and Soviet women pilots during World War II.

In the pages to follow, Amy Goodpaster Strebe will transport you into the extraordinary lives of the world's first women military pilots—to help you better understand what motivated these heroic female aviators to risk their lives in "Freedom's fight."

Trish Beckman
Commander, U.S. Navy (Retired)

ACKNOWLEDGMENTS

There are numerous people to whom I am indebted for their assistance with this book. I am particularly grateful to Dr. Mary Pickering, professor of history at San Jose State University, in whose women's history course I initially learned of the Soviet women combat pilots of World War II. I am also thankful to her for overseeing the writing of my master's thesis, from which this book originated.

Thank you to all of the Women Airforce Service Pilots (WASP) who have generously taken the time over the years to share their stories with me. You are America's greatest treasures. Special thanks go to WASP Florence Shutsy-Reynolds, who took me under her wing at the WASP reunion in Portland, Oregon, and kindly introduced me to her friends. Big thanks to Nancy Parrish, director of Wings Across America, and to her mother, WASP Deanie Bishop Parrish, for their kindness and assistance with this book. I am tremendously grateful to Trish Beckman for graciously agreeing to write the foreword and to Gen. Chuck Yeager and Maj. Nicole Malachowski for their kind support of this project.

I am thankful to Dawn Letson and Tracey MacGowan at Texas Woman's University's Blagg-Huey Library for helping me to locate documents and photographs of the WASP in The Woman's Collection. I am especially indebted to Hugh Munro Neely of Timeline Films, who very generously shared his photographs of the Soviet women veterans. Thank you to Holly Reed at the National Archives and Lonna McKinley at the National Museum of the U.S. Air Force for their assistance in locating photographs of the WASP for this book.

I am grateful to the editorial staff at Potomac Books, Inc., in particular Elizabeth Demers, Claire Noble, and Kathryn Owens. A big thank you goes to my friends Katya Shirokova Gubenko and Kim Green for coming to my rescue on more than one occasion when I needed help with a Russian translation. Большое спасибо!

My heartfelt appreciation goes to the Russian women veterans of World War II. To Ekaterina K. Polunina, regimental historian and senior aircraft mechanic in the 586th Fighter Aviation Regiment; to my friend Elena Kulkova, Pe-2 dive bomber pilot in the 125th Guards Dive Bomber Aviation Regiment, for her friendship and hospitality during my trip to Moscow; to Galina Brok-Beltsova, navigator in the 125th Guards Dive Bomber Aviation Regiment; and to all my Aviatrissa friends in Russia, thank you for sharing your history and love of country with me. Благодарю Вас от всего сердца. Я Вас всех очень уважаю и люблю! Вы мои героини.

I owe the utmost gratitude to my parents, Larry and Valerie Goodpaster. Thank you from the bottom of my heart for your continued love and support in all that I do. I am blessed to be married to an incredibly supportive husband. Gary, thank you for your unwavering patience and encouragement all these years. Lastly, I would like to acknowledge my children, Abbie and Spencer, who inspire me each and every day. May you always have the courage to follow your dreams, wherever they may take you.

ABBREVIATIONS

ATA	Air Transport Auxiliary
ATC	Air Transport Command
CAA	Civil Aeronautics Administration
OWI	Officer of War Information
USAAF	United States Army Air Forces
USAF	United States Air Force
WAAC	Women's Army Auxiliary Corps
WAC	Women's Army Corps
WAFS	Women's Auxiliary Ferrying Squadron
WASP	Women Airforce Service Pilots
WFTD	Women's Flying Training Detachment

INTRODUCTION

In 1941, two events took place on opposite sides of the world that forever impacted the history of women in aviation. On the morning of June 22, 1941, the Germans invaded the Soviet Union in the form of Hitler's Operation Barbarossa. In the early morning hours of December 7, 1941, the Japanese attacked the American naval base at Pearl Harbor, thus inciting the United States to join World War II. Thousands of American and Soviet citizens, fueled by patriotism, eagerly volunteered for the armed forces.

From the onset neither country could anticipate the tremendous human as well as material resources that would be required to win the war. The international conflict provided opportunities to serve that were unprecedented in history. For the first time the United States and the Soviet Union recruited women pilots to fly military aircraft for their countries. The United States, under the tutelage of Jacqueline Cochran, formed the WASP (Women Airforce Service Pilots) program, where over one thousand women flyers ferried aircraft from factories to airbases throughout the United States and Canada from 1942 to 1944. The WASP flew every type of aircraft and, aside from combat, performed every duty inside the cockpit as their male counterparts. Thirty-eight WASP gave their lives in the service of their country. In the three years the WASP program was activated, the female flyers logged sixty million miles and flew 80 percent of all ferrying missions in the war.

In the Soviet Union, Marina Raskova, famous for her historic 1938 flight to the Far East, put a similar program into place. She was also one of the first women to receive the Hero of the Soviet Union award. Equivalent to the U.S. Medal of Honor, it is the highest award the country bestowed upon its citizens who were singled out for exemplary acts of bravery. In October

1941, she formed the all-female 122nd Composite Air Group that trained pilots, navigators, mechanics, and ground crew for three new regiments: the 586th Fighter Aviation Regiment, the 587th Day Bomber Aviation Regiment, and the 588th Night Bomber Aviation Regiment. A little over one thousand women flew a combined total of more than thirty-thousand combat sorties, producing at least thirty Heroes of the Soviet Union, including at least two fighter aces. More than fifty airwomen are believed to have been killed in action. Two of the regiments received the elite "Guards" appellation.[1]

Despite the differences in their aerial operations and military status throughout the war, the American and Soviet women pilots had much in common. Both groups of pilots shared a deep love of flying and a desire to help their countries defeat the scourge of fascism. The women, many of whom were in their late teens and early twenties, were patriotic, idealistic, and determined. Yet, despite the official support of the women pilots by the air force, the flyers of both nations faced discrimination, from the mistrust and prejudices of male pilots and military personnel, as well as from the physical challenges and training. The women formed close relationships because of the dangers of flying and the deaths of their fellow pilots. After the war, the WASP—deactivated in 1944—found themselves excluded from postwar aviation. It took thirty-three years, not until 1977, for them to achieve long sought for veteran status. Soviet women pilots were likewise barred from their postwar military as Soviet officials told them to disregard their wartime experiences and return home. Moreover, despite the Russian women's unprecedented opportunity to fly military aircraft during World War II and their achievements in combat, their moment in history was brief and later largely forgotten by the Soviet public once the war came to a close. With peace came the reestablishment of gender stereotypes, and the women pilots in both nations found that their place in society was not in the cockpit of a military airplane, but in the home as wives and mothers. The airwomen had fulfilled a temporary need created by the war and were expected to return to their prewar roles in society. There was seemingly no room for women pilots in postwar military aviation.

On the surface, these women appear remarkably different in their military status, political ideology, and wartime missions. Yet, a surprising link ties these flyers together, not just as military pilots, but also as women forced to endure the same gender stereotypes and prejudices that their unique wartime duties generated.

One WASP described her participation in World War II as "a magical bubble—a lucky accident of history."[2] The women pilots were acutely aware that their unique wartime experiences were short-lived. American women would have to wait more than thirty years before they would be allowed again to fly military aircraft. According to the limited amount of academic literature available on the subject, few if any Russian women military pilots have had the opportunity to fly in combat in the six decades following the end of World War II.[3]

On the European continent at the outbreak of war, thousands of women joined auxiliaries and actively supported their countries' war efforts. As early as 1940, British, Canadian, and Polish women pilots in Great Britain were ferrying military aircraft from factories to air bases for the British Ferry Command and ATA (Air Transport Auxiliary). Having started out with only eight women pilots in 1940 that number increased to 110 during the five years the ATA was in service. Before Pearl Harbor some two hundred American male pilots flew for the ATA. According to WASP Kay Gott, the men and women of the ATA came from a total of twenty-eight countries.[4]

Despite Hitler's distaste for women in the German military, 450,000 joined the women's auxiliaries, in addition to nursing units.[5] Although no women pilots were permitted to fly in combat for the Third Reich, half a dozen female aviators reportedly flew ferrying missions in the Luftwaffe. One of these women was Beate Uhse, who ferried Junkers Ju 87 Stukas and Messerschmitt 109s to the front. Despite the women pilots' noncombat status, one could only imagine the skies above Germany to be a dangerous place for any pilot, regardless of his or her mission. Following the war, Uhse went on to found the world's first sex shop in Flensburg, Germany in 1962. Today her name is associated with Germany's most successful erotica chain, Beate Uhse AG. Uhse remained chairwoman of her company until her death in 2001.[6] Hanna Reitsch, the first woman in history to fly a helicopter in 1938, was accepted into the Luftwaffe as a test pilot.

The only woman flyer who is believed to have flown in combat in the late 1930s before the start of the war is Turkey's first female combat pilot, Sabiha Gökçen, the adopted daughter of Kemal Atatürk, the founder of the Republic of Turkey. Virtually unknown in the West, Gökçen, who died in 2001, reportedly earned numerous international awards for her bravery and flying skills. One of Istanbul's airports was named in her honor.

CHAPTER 1

America's First Women Military Pilots

This is not a time for women to be patient. We are in a war and we need to fight it with all our ability and every weapon possible. Women pilots, in this particular case, are a weapon waiting to be used.
—Eleanor Roosevelt (September 1, 1942)[1]

In the 1930s, a pilot by the name of Jacqueline Cochran became known for her outstanding achievements in the field of aviation. Born Bessie Mae Pittman on May 11, 1905 near Muscogee, Florida, Cochran exhibited a tremendous drive to succeed and was determined to overcome a childhood fraught with poverty.[2] An orphan, she reportedly did not own a pair of shoes until she was eight years old. Cochran would later write of herself, "I might have been born in a hovel, but I was determined to travel with the wind and the stars."[3]

Always looking to reinvent herself, Cochran reportedly picked her new name out of the telephone directory. In her mid-20s, she moved to New York City to work at an upscale beauty salon called Antoine's inside Saks Fifth Avenue and to start her own cosmetics business. At a party, she met millionaire businessman Floyd Odlum to whom she confided her dreams and aspirations. The young Jackie mesmerized him, and on May 10, 1936, the two married.[4] Before tying the knot, Odlum suggested to Cochran that she take flying lessons so she could get around the country faster, selling her cosmetics. Cochran took his advice and earned her pilot's license in only two-and-a-half weeks. In her autobiography, Cochran described her first flying lesson in 1932: "I showed up at Roosevelt Field, Long Island, at the flying school. At that moment, when I paid for my first lesson, a beauty operator ceased to exist and an aviator was born."[5]

Cochran went on to set more speed, distance, and altitude records than any other pilot of her time, male or female—even more than her friend Amelia Earhart, whom she met in 1935 when the two competed in the Bendix Trophy Race, which two years before, had been open only to men. Neither woman won in 1935. But in 1938, Jackie won first prize, beating every man in the race.[6]

On December 4, 1937, Cochran set a new national transcontinental record—beating Howard Hughes's earlier accomplishment—by racing from New York City to Miami in only four hours and twelve minutes.[7] The flight was a dangerous one, but taking risks became Cochran's hallmark. That same year the International League of Aviators voted Cochran the world's outstanding pilot, an award that she went on to win for three consecutive years.[8]

In March 1939, Cochran won her second Harmon Trophy, the highest award given to any aviator in America. The day before the Harmon Award was announced, she had broken a women's altitude record by climbing to 33,000 feet above sea level. Over the next few months Cochran broke two women's records, two national speed records, and one intercity record between Burbank and San Francisco. On each of her record-breaking flights, sustained only with a half-filled bottle of Coca-Cola (a full one would explode at high altitudes) and a fistful of lollipops for "dry mouth," she tested new types of oxygen masks, engine superchargers, sparkplugs, airplane fuel, and wing designs, which would soon appear in America's air arsenal.[9]

That same year the CAA (Civil Aeronautics Administration) began a program of pilot cadet training in American colleges, and many young women enthusiastically signed up for flying lessons. By June 1941, more than 2,000 women pilots across the country had learned to fly. That same month, however, women were dropped from the program to make room for more men, as America's involvement in the war became imminent.[10]

By September 1939, there was little doubt about the Axis powers' intentions to wage total war in Europe. In March, Hitler invaded Czechoslovakia and helped Franco's forces defeat the Republicans in Spain. A month later, Mussolini stormed into Albania. On September 1, German tank divisions rolled into Poland, and the world was again at war. With the conquest of Poland, Hitler also gave the world notice that its next war would be fought largely from the air. The invading ground troops were supported by aerial bombing, part of the *Blitzkrieg*. After a month of intense fighting, Warsaw capitulated on September 27.[11]

Cochran sensed early in the war that women would be needed as pilots, and she eagerly sought the opportunity to bring female aviators into the war effort. She recalled in *The Stars at Noon:*

The pressure on our manpower during World War II and the increasing use of war power made it certain that eventually there would be a need for women pilots. All my war work up until the time General [Hap] Arnold called me home from England [where she was assisting with the Air Transport Auxiliary] had been in preparation for this time of need.[12]

In late September, Cochran wrote a letter to Eleanor Roosevelt. Given the dramatic events happening in Europe, it was not too soon to begin thinking about the idea of utilizing American women pilots in noncombat roles, thus releasing men for combat duty overseas. The effective use of women pilots, Cochran argued "requires organization in advance."[13] She intended to organize such a group of female pilots. The First Lady thanked Cochran for her letter and assured her of women's contributions in the war should the need arise. Ultimately, Roosevelt's influence and support of women's causes helped to facilitate the establishment of the WASP program.

In March 1941, Cochran attended an aviation awards ceremony at the White House and met General H.H. "Hap" Arnold, chief of the U.S. Army Air Corps, and Clayton Knight, who directed American recruiting efforts for the British ATA. After Congress signed the Lend-Lease Act into law on March 11, 1941, the ATA had the authority to ship or fly planes to England. With every possible qualified pilot involved in combat, the British ATA was desperate for recruits from neutral nations. The organization had even enlisted some of Britain's women pilots to ferry planes around the United Kingdom. But the transoceanic hops necessary to deliver the bombers, Knight told Cochran, were proving to be a fearsome deterrent to his recruitment efforts.

Cochran offered Knight her help, and it was not long before she was piloting a Lockheed Hudson bomber from Montreal to ATA headquarters in Prestwick, Scotland, becoming the first woman to pilot a bomber over the North Atlantic.[14] Cochran recruited a group of twenty-five American women pilots to serve in the British ATA and accompanied them to England for training with the British women pilots, who were already ferrying aircraft. While abroad, Cochran formulated a plan to create a similar program in the United States for women flyers.

Upon her return home to the United States in July 1941, Cochran was asked what she was doing in England, and she replied, "I wanted to check up on what those girls were doing, and see how we could organize a similar group in this country."[15] That same month Cochran was invited to lunch with President Roosevelt at Hyde Park, and before she left, she was presented with a letter of introduction to Robert A. Lovett, then Assistant Secretary of War for Air. In the note, the President gave instructions that Cochran was to research a plan for an organization of women pilots to serve with the USAAF (U.S. Army Air Forces).

While Cochran was busy lobbying Washington to create the first women's military flying program in the United States, another well-known female aviator was quietly working on a plan to include women pilots in the war. Twenty-seven-year-old Nancy Harkness Love was a well-connected and highly experienced pilot who was married to Colonel Robert Love, deputy chief of the ATC (Air Transport Command). Nancy Love wrote to Colonel Robert Olds, who was then head of the Air Corps' Ferry Command, with a proposition similar to Cochran's, to enlist fifty to sixty women with extensive flying experience (at least 500 hours logged and a commercial pilot's license) to ferry aircraft from factories to points of embarkation.[16]

Cochran and Love could not have been more different in their personalities and personal ambitions. Cochran was determined, aggressive by nature, and persuasive. Despite her humble beginnings and lack of a formal education, Cochran learned to speak the USAAF's language and was unbending in her resolve to incorporate women flyers into the military's war machine. Love, on the other hand, was a child of privilege. She was bright, well educated, and tenacious but sought only to join and influence the ATC, not to create an entirely new women's flying program, as Cochran planned. In contrast, Cochran desired full control, while Love was satisfied relinquishing many of the chief administrative duties for more time in the cockpit. Despite the differences in the two women's understanding and use of power, they were somehow able to work together for two and a half turbulent years, though they seldom met face-to-face.[17]

Marion Stegeman Hodgson discussed the power struggle that existed between Love and Cochran in a book she wrote about her years as a WASP: "It was one of the minor miracles of the war that these two women, so totally different in background and approach, were eventually able to serve effectively as leaders under the same umbrella, with Jackie emerging as boss lady. Absolutely the only thing they had in common was their love of flying and a driving ambition to use women pilots in the war effort."[18]

Love pushed for an elite group of women pilots on a squadron level to join either the ATC or Ferry Command as an auxiliary unit attached to the Air Corps. Cochran recommended the establishment of a complete, full-fledged women's flying training program, under her direction, geared to produce thousands of ferry pilots. Initially, successful applicants would be American citizens between the ages of twenty-one and thirty-five who had a minimum of 200 hours of flying time.[19] Later on the age requirement was lowered to eighteen and one-half years, and flying time was reduced to seventy-five hours. The women were also required to stand at least sixty inches tall and pass the high standards of the Form Sixty-Four physical examination by a flight surgeon.[20] Later in the program the height regulations were raised to sixty-four inches. The initial program called for twenty-three weeks of training, including 115 hours of flying and 180 hours of ground school. Although Cochran ultimately prevailed, Love succeeded in creating the WAFS (Women's Auxiliary Ferrying Squadron), whose members would be the first to ferry aircraft from the factories to the air bases. The twenty-eight original WAFS had an average of 1,100 hours of flying time when they were accepted into the program.[21]

Upon learning of Love's new group of women ferrying pilots, Cochran convinced General Arnold that in light of the attack on Pearl Harbor and America's entrance into the war, more women pilots were needed than the WAFS could supply. Arnold agreed, and on November 16, 1942, Cochran established the WFTD (Women's Flying Training Detachment) at Howard Hughes Airport in Houston, Texas, with an initial class of twenty-five women, who were required to have 200 hours of flying and a commercial pilot's license. The mission of the WFTD was to perform whatever flight duties the USAAF required within the United States. Like the WAFS, these pilots ferried planes, but they also tested and flew aircraft reported to have mechanical problems; delivered planes in need of fixing to repair depots; performed check flights on repaired planes; broke in new engines; towed targets for antiaircraft gunnery practice; flew searchlight tracking missions; simulated bombing, strafing, and smoke-laying missions for troop training; moved aircraft from base to base; towed gliders, and instructed male pilot cadets.

When the classes outgrew their existing facility, Cochran's women pilots moved to Avenger Field in Sweetwater, Texas. The new training base was located 200 miles west of Dallas-Fort Worth. Sweetwater was small, dry, isolated, and wide open—the perfect place Cochran thought to train her women pilots to fly planes the Army way.

Once Cochran had the facilities and a base of trained women instructors, she began accepting women flight cadets into an intensive training program. The applicants, required to be experienced pilots, were found largely from a list maintained by the CAA of the country's 3,000 licensed women pilots.[22] As word leaked out about the women's flying program, applications from all over the country poured into Cochran's office, totaling over 25,000. Women from a variety of backgrounds—actresses, secretaries, dancers, college students, nurses, mothers, and socialites—eagerly applied. Ultimately, 1,830 pilots were accepted into pilot training.[23]

On August 5, 1943, the WAFS and the WFTD merged to form the WASP with Cochran as director of the WASP and its training division and Love as director of the Ferrying Division. In the twenty-five months the WASP program was in existence, 1,074 women successfully completed the grueling six-month training program at Avenger Field and earned their silver wings.

Despite the WASP's nonmilitary status, the women were required to adhere to Army regulations. They slept in barracks six to a room, with twelve sharing a single bathroom. "There was no privacy—none at all," remembered WASP Marty Martin Wyall. "We just learned to live together."[24] The all-women's air base created a sensation, and in the first few weeks over 100 hundred planes with male crews reported mysterious engine problems and requested emergency landings on Avenger Field. Cochran promptly banned all unauthorized landings, and Avenger Field became known as "Cochran's Convent."[25]

For the newly arrived women pilots, this was the chance of a lifetime. Hodgson reported for pilot training at Avenger Field in March 1943 and recalled her first impressions in her book *Winning My Wings: A Woman Airforce Service Pilot in World War II:* "We were a disparate group in our civilian clothes as we paraded in an unmilitary fashion, out of step, toward the hangar. I felt like giggling at our ragtag appearance as we passed a neat formation of coverall-clad female trainees in perfect step, the rhythmic cadence of their feet keeping time with the lusty song they were singing. Excitement swept over me at the thought that I'd soon be one of them—sunburned, disciplined, fit, happy, purposeful."[26]

The WASP, like many women in wartime America, yearned to do something meaningful to help the war effort. The unprecedented opportunity for these women to fly military aircraft for their country gave the pilots a unique sense of pride and purpose, and they welcomed the chance to do their part for Uncle Sam.

Juliette Jenner Stege was a successful dancer on Broadway before becoming a WASP. "My friends in show business tried to convince me not to join the WASP," said Stege, who graduated in the 44-W-3 class. "They would say to me, 'you're just a dumb chorus girl—you're going to get yourself killed.'"[27] Stege ignored her friends' advice and took flying lessons on Long Island. "It's important to learn not to say no," she told this author at the WASP's 64th anniversary reunion in Portland, Oregon. "You have to take risks in life."[28]

The trainees were awakened every morning at 6:00 a.m. by the sounds of Reveille. After breakfast their day would be spent in physical training, ground school, (which included instruction in mathematics, physics, map reading, charts, navigation, engines, weather, code and communications), and flying. The pilots received over 210 hours of military flight training at Avenger Field.[29]

For flying, the WASP were issued men's flight suits that were many sizes too large for them. "Surplus Army mechanics' olive drab overalls, size forty-four and up, dubbed 'zoot suits' replaced our civilian clothes, while cosmetics and fancy hairstyles became relics of the past,"[30] WASP Doris Brinker Tanner later wrote. Adaline Blank, a trainee in the WASP class 43-W-8, wrote a letter home to her sister describing life at Avenger Field:

The whole set-up and the very atmosphere is ARMY. We "fall in" and march to everything; to the flight line, to classes, to drill, to "mess." Every day after lunch we have an hour's drill under this boiling Texas sun...tomorrow we begin our flying in the Fairchild PT-19, our primary trainer ship. I can hardly wait to get my hands on a real ship ...already my big worry is that I might "wash out." It's going to be plenty tough to come up to Army standards. Many of the girls have had much more preliminary work than I have, and much more flying time. Several from W-7 "washed" today. Everyone gets depressed when they go...tonight the Recreation Room was like a morgue— you just can't help wondering "will I be next?" [31]

WASP Florence Shutsy-Reynolds, known to her friends as "Shutsy," reported to Avenger Field on December 7, 1943. She recalled her training days with the class of 44-W-5. "There were six of us in a bay including a debutante, a housewife, an artist who specialized in Chinese art, and a school teacher," she said. "Two washed out, two washed out to another class, and two graduated."[32]

The fear of every WASP trainee was "washing out" of the program. It was a genuine fear too, as only the best pilots went on to earn their wings. Jean Hascall Cole recalled the washouts in her class of 44-W-2 in her memoirs:

Most of the heartbreaking washouts took place during those first two months of training...Marge Gilbert was next door to me, but Carol White had washed out early in training. She was in tears, as I remember, and we felt sorry for her, but we felt lucky at the same time that we were still there. There seemed to be so much "luck" involved in the washouts. We later found out that many good pilots didn't make it. [33]

After many months of military pilot training, the WASP sighed a big sigh of relief once graduation day arrived. Each class composed and sang a special song in tribute to the departing graduates. One favorite parodied "Yankee Doodle Dandy":

We are Yankee Doodle pilots,
Yankee Doodle do or die;
Real live nieces of our Uncle Sam,
Born with a yearning to fly.
Keep in step to all our classes,
March to flight line with our pals;
Yankee Doodle came to Texas
Just to fly the PTs,
We are those Yankee Doodle gals.[34]

The female pilots reportedly caught the attention of Walt Disney, and he had the artists at Walt Disney Studios design a cartoon mascot for the WASP. Most U.S. military units in World War II had cartoon mascots, which decorated everything from jackets to bombers. The WASP's "Fifi-nella" or "Fifi" as she was nicknamed, came from the children's book *The Gremlins* written in 1942 by Roald Dahl, who was at the time a young Royal Air Force pilot. His book told of imaginary creatures that played tricks on pilots. He named male mischief makers "gremlins"; a female one was a "Fifinella" or "Fifi." WASP felt Fifi was not as mischievous as a male gremlin. "She kept the sand out of your gas tank and kept the engine running," said Nonie Horton Anderson. Betty Jane ("B.J.") Williams added, "Fifi helped us come home safely." [35]

Following graduation, the WASP were dispersed to air bases throughout the country, where they took up assignments transporting aircraft across the United States and into Canada. The women pilots operated from 110 facilities and flew more than sixty million miles in seventy-eight different types of aircraft, from the smallest trainers to the fastest fighters and the largest bombers. They ferried the bulk of new aircraft from the factories to training bases and embarkation points, and flew combat-weary planes to repair depots, then did the after-service checkout, often when male pilots would not. They towed targets for live ammunition antiaircraft battery practice, as well as air-to-air gunnery. The WASP conducted weather reconnaissance and participated in smoke-laying missions during maneuvers. They were employed as instructors and did everything from radio-controlled and instrument test flying to thousands of engineering tests and utility tests. [36]

Some graduates, like Ann Baumgartner Carl, became test pilots. Many WASP also went on to pursuit training where they learned to fly fighters like the North American P-51 Mustang, while others became qualified to fly in bombers like the B-17 Flying Fortress and B-29 Superfortress. Twenty-two-year-old Dora Dougherty Strother was one of only two WASP chosen to fly the colossal B-29.

Lieutenant Colonel Paul W. Tibbets, Jr. (who later piloted the *Enola Gay* that dropped the first atomic bomb on Hiroshima, Japan) recruited Strother and Dorothea "Didi" Johnson Moorman to fly the massive bomber to demonstrate to the male pilots that it could be flown. Tibbets was determined to prove to these men that not only could the B-29 be flown but that it could also be flown by women. [37] The women were given only three days training in Birmingham, Alabama to learn how to fly the heavy bomber. After an anxious check ride when one of the engines caught on fire, the WASP successfully flew the B-29 (christened *Ladybird*) to Clovis Army Air Field in New Mexico. In 1995, Strother received a letter from a male pilot who was on that historic flight:

I realize that it was a long time ago but I want to thank you for helping me that day at Clovis. You came to show us that the B-29 plane was not one to be feared. You were the pilot that day and you

demonstrated your excellent flying skills and convinced us that the
B-29 was a plane that any pilot would be proud to fly. From that day
on we never had a pilot who didn't want to fly the B-29.[38]

With each new success, Cochran was convinced that her WASP were
making a difference in the war. It troubled Cochran, however, that her
women pilots were still considered only volunteer civil servants with no official military status. With General Arnold's backing, Cochran helped to
reintroduce a bill to Congress to make the WASP a woman's service within
the USAAF. (The first bill that was introduced in September 1943 was
ignored.) On June 21, 1944, HR4219 (named the Costello Bill after
Representative John Costello of California who introduced it) was defeated
by nineteen votes, despite vigorous lobbying efforts by Arnold and Cochran.
Not since the beginning of the war in 1941 had any legislation supported by
the Army Air Forces been turned down.[39]

There are many reasons for the defeat of the WASP militarization bill. By
early 1944, air superiority had been achieved in Europe, and American male
pilots began returning home. Flying schools were being shut down so civilian pilots were now faced with the draft—not to be pilots, but foot soldiers
in the infantry. If the male pilots took over the WASP's flying jobs, they
could avoid the draft. They launched an aggressive campaign against the
WASP in the media and on Capitol Hill.[40] The protests of the male pilots
coincided with a growing backlash against the idea of women "freeing
men to fight" as men returned home from the war to find women in coveted
flying positions. Newspaper accounts from this period illustrate how tradi-
tionalists both in and out of Congress were becoming increasingly concerned about women's growing independence and economic power and
feared they would not return to their "rightful" roles of homemaker,
mother, and low-wage employee when the war ended. These factors,
accompanied by tremendous social pressures facilitated by the media, constituted a powerful lobby against passage of the bill that sought to militarize
the WASP.

The defeat of the Costello Bill meant that the WASP would remain civil
servants without the benefits given to full-fledged members of the United
States military. The WASP were denied benefits under the GI Bill, including
life insurance, medical coverage, education assistance, and home mortgages.
It was not until 1977 that President Jimmy Carter granted the WASP veteran
status. The WASP felt the sting of their quasi-military status directly whenever a fellow pilot was killed. Because they had not been officially accepted
into the Army Air Forces, the government refused to pay for the bodies of
WASP to be shipped home for burial or pay for funeral expenses. The
women pilots often had to collect the necessary funds themselves.

In order to appreciate the exceptional opportunity for women pilots to fly
military aircraft during the war, it is helpful to look back a decade earlier to

the 1930s. The Great Depression cast a long shadow over the 1940s. According to Susan M. Hartmann in her book *The Home Front and Beyond: American Women in the 1940s,* when the economy hit its low point in 1933 the gross national product plunged from $149.3 to $107.6 billion; national income stood at one-half its 1929 level; and more than 30 percent of the workforce—twelve million men and women—could not find employment.[41]

The majority of adult women experienced the Depression years as wives and not paid workers. More than 90 percent of all women married, but only 15 percent of all married women were employed outside the home in 1940.[42] Above all women were viewed as mothers and wives, and their participation outside the home in the public sphere was limited. Especially during the harsh years of the Depression, women were discriminated against if they were married and decided to seek employment. Public opinion viewed these workingwomen as stealing jobs away from able-bodied men who needed to work to support their families. A Gallup poll in 1936 reported that 82 percent of the respondents believed that wives with employed husbands should not work outside the home and that three-fourths of the women polled agreed.[43]

The outbreak of war in 1941 helped to solve America's domestic economic troubles while boosting production and creating new jobs. As thousands of men left their jobs to join the military and were deployed overseas, women were encouraged to leave their homes (if only temporarily) to replace the men in the labor force. The United States government reminded women of their duty to their country, and they entered the workplace in large numbers. While the Depression had encouraged public criticism of women workers, the labor shortage of the war years necessitated appeals by government and employers for women to take jobs. The need for female labor lent a new legitimacy to the women worker and made government, employers, and labor unions more willing to think about their concerns. Between 1940 and 1945 the female labor force grew by more than 50 percent.[44] Despite a willingness to deviate from the established norms for women, the claims of home and family remained strong. Wives of servicemen were three times as likely to work as wives with their husbands present. The women, some of whom were employed for the first time outside of their homes, felt pride in their accomplishments. An older woman in Baltimore who had returned to paid employment after years of being a homemaker, commented on her job in assembly work at Bendix Friez Company: "I love my job and I hate the idea of giving it up. Sometimes I can hardly wait to get there. Never thought I could do such exacting work—and I'm real proud." [45]

Women with special skills were sought in every aspect of war work, and the few thousand women in the United States, who had experience in aviation as pilots, were recruited to do their part as well. Women flying enthusiasts, who at the time had to be content flying for recreational purposes or working as a flight instructor, jumped at the rare opportunity to fly military aircraft while also contributing to the war effort. The women who joined the WASP knew they were an elite group and they were determined to prove that they were just as capable of flying military planes as their male counterparts.

Unfortunately, the women pilots did not have long to prove their merit in the cockpit. The WASP program was cut short when it was officially terminated on December 20, 1944, eight months before the war ended. It was the first of the women's services to be disbanded. In the words of WASP Doris Brinker Tanner, "The battle to give women equal opportunity in military cockpits was lost." [46] Although the airwomen proved that the experiment had been successful, the WASP program could not hold up under the social pressure brought on by negative publicity in the media and a powerful lobby of male civilian pilots who wanted the women pilots' jobs. After a lengthy battle for militarization, General Arnold and Cochran were forced to accept defeat. The stunned WASP packed their bags and returned home, while planes remained at airfields across America waiting to be delivered until male pilots could be trained to replace them.

Despite criticism of the WASP program that developed in the media as a result of their attempt to militarize while male pilots returned from overseas duty, the women flyers earned the respect of male pilots as well as many topranking military officers. In the end, they proved that women were physically capable of piloting military aircraft. General Arnold, a staunch supporter of the WASP, was the keynote speaker at the graduation of the last class on December 7, 1944:

> We will not again look upon a women's flying organization as experimental. We will know that they can handle our fastest fighters, our heaviest bombers; we will know that they are capable of ferrying, target towing, flying training, test flying, and the countless other activities which you have proved you can do...we of the Army Air Force are proud of you; we will never forget our debt to you. [47]

The backlash of official government action against the WASP hurt the pilots profoundly and bewildered them, but they clung to the knowledge that their service record had been outstanding. Some of the women pilots were later commissioned in the new United States Air Force, but not on flying status. The majority of the WASP married, started families, or returned to college or their prewar jobs. Although there were some who continued flying after the war, the Women Airforce Service Pilots forever cherished the memories of their days as America's first female military pilots.

CHAPTER 2

Marina Raskova and Her Soviet Aviation Regiments

She [Raskova] said to Stalin, "You know, they are running away to the front all the same, they are taking things into their own hands, and it will be worse, you understand if they steal airplanes to go." ...And we had just an incident. There were several girls who had asked to go to the front, and they were turned down. So they stole a fighter plane and flew off to the front. They just couldn't wait....And because of this, they formed first a group, then three aviation regiments.

—Yevgeniya Zhigulenko (Pilot, 46th Guards Night Bomber Aviation Regiment)[1]

Thousands of miles away another accomplished woman flyer was preparing to organize a group of young female pilots to defend Soviet Russia. Marina Raskova, one of the most venerated and best-loved women aviators of the USSR, is largely unknown in the West. Raskova is admired for her achievements in aviation the same way Amelia Earhart is in the United States. Founder of the world's first all-female air regiments during World War II, Raskova, who rose to the rank of major, became the first woman navigator in the Soviet Union and commanding officer of the 587th Day Bomber Aviation Regiment, subsequently renamed after her death, in 1943, the 125th M.M. Raskova *Borisov* Guards Bomber Aviation Regiment. One of the first women to earn the prestigious title Hero of the Soviet Union, Raskova served as a role model for her fellow aviators, male and female, not only for her tremendous skill and personal courage, but also for her ability to make decisions and lead under severe and often difficult circumstances.

Like Jacqueline Cochran, Raskova did not set out to become a pilot. Born in Moscow on March 28, 1912, Marina Mikhailovna Malinina aspired to be an opera singer, but a middle-ear infection at the age of fifteen pushed her life down another path. Raskova chose instead to study chemistry and engineering, and later mastered the theory of air navigation. She became the first woman in the USSR to earn the diploma of professional air navigator, going on to become an instructor at N. Ye. Zhukovsky Air Force Engineering Academy in Moscow.[2]

As an instructor, Raskova taught military navigation to male officers who, although initially skeptical of her knowledge and abilities, later admitted that they were now convinced of women's capabilities in aviation. The Academy rewarded Raskova by sending her to the Central Flying Club at Tushino, near Moscow, for flying lessons, which she completed in August 1935. After her training, Raskova became an instrument flying instructor and taught advanced navigation for command personnel.

By the mid-1930s, Raskova became involved in a greater number of important aviation-related events, and in August 1935, she took part in her first independent flight as a pilot. According to Kazimiera J. Cottam in her book *Women in War and Resistance: Selected Biographies of Soviet Women Soldiers,* in July 1936, Raskova began probationary navigator training in the 23rd Heavy Air Brigade.[3] In the meantime, she continued teaching at the Academy. In June 1937, Raskova participated as navigator in an air race from Moscow to Sevastopol and back to Moscow flying the same plane as in the 1935 flight but this time with additional fuel tanks. She was the fourth to arrive in Sevastopol and the sixth to return to Moscow, completing the journey within twenty-four hours. That same year Raskova met pilot Valentina Grizodubova who proposed to her that they fly together in a Yak-12 to establish a long distance record. On October 24, 1937, they set a new women's record when they covered approximately 895 miles from Moscow to Aktyubinsk, Kazakhstan.[4]

On July 2, 1938, Raskova again established a new women's long distance record when she flew (as navigator) with pilot Polina Osipenko and copilot Vera Lomako in an MP-1 nonstop from the Black Sea to the White Sea, having taken off in Sevastopol and landed in the vicinity of Arkhangel'sk on Lake Kholmovskoye. The route lay across four different air masses—tropical, continental, polar, and arctic—and required tremendous skills by the crew. The aviators set an international women's straight-line distance record when they flew 3,695 miles. As a result of this record-setting flight, senior lieutenants Osipenko and Lomako as well as lieutenant Raskova (who became a career officer in 1938) were awarded the Order of Lenin.[5]

Not long after this flight, Grizodubova, with Stalin's support, arranged for an aircraft to be assigned to them for their proposed flight to the Far East (with Osipenko as copilot). It was an ANT-37 (a converted long-range DB-2 bomber) nicknamed *Rodina* ("Motherland") by Grizodubova. In addition to flight training, the three women practiced firing rifles and pistols. The flight was delayed after Raskova developed appendicitis, and in September 1938, a state commission cancelled the flight because of the lateness in the year and anticipated bad weather. Stalin, however, overruled the decision, and the *Rodina* took off on September 24, 1938, at 8:16 a.m.[6]

During the course of this mission, overcast skies completely obscured all visual landmarks, leaving radio signals as the only means of orientation. When the radio station ceased transmitting, there was nothing to do but continue on, eventually running out of fuel. Raskova's crew position in the nose of the aircraft was hazardous for a crash landing, so she was ordered to parachute from the plane over the *taiga,* a dense, swampy, forested area of Siberia. Raskova landed in the swamp, and it was not until ten days later that she finally came upon her aircraft and was reunited with Osipenko and Grizodubova. The story of Raskova's flight was widely publicized, and her courage and stamina caught the imagination of the Soviet people.[7]

Raskova spent several months recovering from the leg injuries she sustained as a result of the historic flight. Not only had Raskova proven her courage and skill in flying, but her youthful beauty also helped to attract the interest of the Russian people. At the age of twenty-six she was a national celebrity, a recipient of the second Order of Lenin, as well as the Gold Star of Hero of the Soviet Union. Raskova, along with Grizodubova and Osipenko, became the first women to receive the country's highest honor and the only women to receive it before the war. The flyers were elevated to the equivalent status of American movie idols in the USSR, and they received significant attention from the press. Despite women's involvement in the field of aviation since the early days of balloon flight in the late eighteenth-century, the world had not yet grown accustomed to reading about the exploits of female pilots. The Soviet public was entranced by these women flyers, who despite their feminine nature, had excelled in the male-dominated field of aviation. Stalin toasted Raskova, Grizodubova, and Osipenko at a banquet held in their honor at the Kremlin. In his speech he remarked on the history of matriarchy in Russia, and he concluded by saying, "Today these three women have avenged the heavy centuries of the oppression of women."[8] According to author David L. Hoffmann, Soviet propaganda in the 1930s depicted heroines as both valiant workers and dutiful mothers. Even Soviet pilot-heroines were portrayed as both pilots and mothers, and at the Kremlin reception to honor them, Hoffmann pointed out that the female aviators were pictured with their children and described as devoted mothers.[9]

Raskova would come to inspire hundreds of young women to fly for the Soviet Union when the time came to defend it. In Reina Pennington's book *Wings, Women, and War: Soviet Airwomen in World War II Combat,* pilot Yevgeniya Zhigulenko recalled Raskova before the war: "Marina Raskova was an exceptional person. A famous pilot and Hero of the Soviet Union, she was still a simple, kind woman. She helped many young women who wanted to fly."[10] Despite her fame and the pressures placed upon her during the war, Raskova was known for her friendliness and her down-to-earth nature. She became the idol of many, including Soviet ace Lidiya Litvyak, who would become the first woman in history to shoot down an enemy aircraft. She reportedly kept pictures of Raskova in her notebook. The aircrew of the *Rodina* met for the last time on March 8, 1939, at the Pilots' Club on International Women's Day. Osipenko was killed two months later in a plane crash. At her funeral, Stalin was one of the pallbearers.

When Germany invaded the Soviet Union on June 22, 1941, Raskova, who was working as a civil defense volunteer at the time, began receiving hundreds of letters from women pilots eager to utilize their flying skills in the war. In October, after getting the full support of Stalin, Raskova set in motion a voluntary recruitment of women flyers, and Aviation Group 122 was born. Historians have several theories as to why Stalin approved the unprecedented formation of the women's air regiments. One theory is that the women were recruited as the result of a presumed shortage of male pilots. Pennington points out that this perception of a shortage of personnel during the war is inaccurate.[11] On the eve of the war the Soviet Air Force was the largest in the world, yet it had a shortage of aircraft. Women's regiments may have also been created solely for propaganda purposes. Lastly, the most credible theory suggests that they were established because of the popularity and persistence of Raskova.

Raskova used her personal relationship with Stalin to convince him that women pilots should be utilized in the war. She also emphasized the young women's strong patriotic feelings and their desire to fulfill their duty to their country. Despite those in the Kremlin who believed that combat was not a woman's affair, Raskova's persistence won out. Before giving her his blessing, however, Stalin reportedly cautioned Raskova, "You understand, future generations will not forgive us for sacrificing young girls."[12]

Three women combat aviation regiments were formed under the auspices of the 122nd Aviation Group: the 586th Fighter Aviation Regiment (Yak-1 fighters) that would later become part of the 270th Bomber Division of the 8th Air Army; the 587th Day Bomber Aviation Regiment (Pe-2 bombers); and the 588th Night Bomber Aviation Regiment (Po-2 biplanes). In February 1943, the 588th was renamed the 46th Guards Night Bomber Aviation Regiment in recognition of its outstanding achievements, and the 587th Regiment became the 125th Guards Bomber Aviation Regiment.

The 46th was the only one of the three original regiments that remained exclusively female throughout the war (the other two regiments incorporated some men.) The regiment flew a total of 24,000 combat missions and was the most decorated of the women's regiments with twenty-three of its members being awarded the Gold Star of the Soviet Union (by 1990), five of them posthumously. The women pilots would later be nicknamed

Nachthexen ("Night Witches") by their German counterparts, who came to fear their successful aerial tactics in the wooden Po-2 planes they flew on night missions.[13] Galina Brok-Beltsova,[14] a navigator in the 125th Guards Bomber Aviation Regiment, explained in an interview after the war, how the women flyers acquired the nickname by the German pilots that has stuck with them ever since.

> We slept in anything we could find—holes in the ground, tents, caves —but the Germans had to have their barracks, you know. They are very precise. So their barracks were built, all in a neat row, and we would come at night, after they were asleep, and bomb them. Of course, they would have to run out into the night in their underwear, and they were probably saying, "Oh, those night witches!" Or maybe they called us something worse. We, of course, would have preferred to have been called "night beauties," but, whichever, we did our job.[15]

One of the Soviet Union's most highly decorated fighter pilots, Alexei Maresyev, praised his country's women pilots who fought and died alongside the men during the Great Patriotic War:

> It is hardly possible to overestimate the contribution made by [Soviet] women to our victory over Nazism...many of them fell on the battlefield, having discharged their soldierly duty honourably. They had a zest for life; they wanted to study, to raise children, and to work hard, but when the need arose they faced danger and died without faltering. They consciously sacrificed their young lives in the great cause...on board fighters and bombers they fought the enemy every bit as well as men did. These Soviet young girls amply demonstrated their iron will, steady hand, and accurate eye.[16]

Nadezhda Popova, a pilot in the 46th Guards Night Bomber Aviation Regiment, recalled several decades after World War II: "Sometimes, on a dark night, I will stand outside my home and peer into the sky, the wind tugging at my hair. I stare into the blackness and I close my eyes, and I imagine myself once more a young girl, up there in my little bomber. And I ask myself, 'Nadya—how did you do it?'"[17]

To put the women pilots' achievements into perspective, it is important to look back at the lives of Soviet women in the decade that preceded the war years. A famous painting by Russian artist Yuri Pimenov entitled *New Moscow* from the 1930s shows a woman driving a car down a street in the capital. The painting suggests her independence, modernity, and competence. She is driving alone, needing no one alongside to give support or advice on how she could improve her driving. Like the "new" Moscow, she is a "new" urban woman, self-determined and capable of adapting her lifestyle to the changing times while at the same time also benefiting from them. She is up to date, has mastered the latest technology of the road, and is moving forward. She personifies the Soviet idea of progress.[18] Most Soviet women in the 1930s of course did not look like the woman in this painting; they possessed no car and had little hope of ever owning one. The painting signified, however, that a new era was dawning and that change was afoot. Gender relations were redefined in a decade where women were then pushed by the Soviet state to increase productivity. As their workload amplified, wages increased for the "new" women. They became part of a labor elite and received monetary and material rewards for their efforts as well as invitations to attend conferences, where they came in contact with top leaders. Competition between female workers spurred them on to even greater productivity. Pilot Osipenko pledged to "fly higher, further and faster than all the girls in the world."[19] The bonuses and rewards given to the women were thought to be incidental, however. Soviet women, it was believed, were not motivated by personal gain but were concerned with the well-being of society as a whole. Soviet citizens, regardless of gender, were expected to sacrifice their individual aspirations for the good of the state. Pilot Grizodubova summed up this view of the female mentality: "Whenever Soviet woman works, she is led by a single aim: to be of use to her beloved motherland."[20]

By the start of the war, Russian women already made up 45 percent of the working force,[21] while in the United States, female workers represented 27.6 percent of America's prewar labor force.[22] The German invasion in June 1941 produced some adjustments to the images of Soviet women. Women took on a new symbolic form. The "new" Soviet woman was replaced by the image of Mother Russia. Instead of driving cars along Moscow's main boulevards, women were now portrayed wearing headscarves and flowing skirts, urging their sons on to battle. According to historian Barbara Evans Clements, in the iconography of the war and also in the minds of many Soviet soldiers, women came to represent endurance, rebirth, and the more nurturing of emotions rarely found in the world of combat. In her article, Clements extended this enduring image to women themselves: "Women as well must have drawn sustenance from this vision of themselves, for it honored their contribution to the war, justified their suffering, and legitimated their own deep feelings about their succoring role within the family and the community."[23] Motherhood was an essential feature of the Soviet woman, and she was encouraged to break records in this field too.

In reality, women not only urged their sons to fight but also took up arms themselves. Nearly one million Soviet women fought in uniform and performed all kinds of combat duties during the war.[24] In contrast, by the end of World War II, approximately 350,000 women had served in the United States military in noncombat roles.[25] For Soviet women during the Great Patriotic War, the image of Mother Russia seemed to embody not only the caring and protective qualities of a mother but also the self-sacrificing and courageous traits of a warrior, defending her country as she would her own child. In the 1930s, and for many years following the war, women would be called upon to work and help rebuild the USSR. The image of the brave and selfless mother who sacrificed and defended her nation against all foes, however, would endure.

The 1930s was not only a decade of rapid industrialization in the Soviet Union, but it was also considered to be the "Golden Age of Aviation." There was a surge in aviation programs, both civilian and military. The second Five-Year Plan called for a tremendous increase in both number and distance of civil aviation routes. Geological surveys and Arctic missions were then conducted by air, and Soviet accomplishments in sport and military aviation received heightened attention.[26] Soviet Russia in the 1930s was complicated and also potentially dangerous. The same system that nurtured women pilots' love of flying and encouraged them to explore aviation was also capable of destroying them in Stalin's totalitarian state.

Because the Soviet Union had the distinction of being the first country in the world to proclaim legal equality for women in 1917, the military flying schools and Osoaviakhim (the Society for Cooperation in Defense and Aviation-Chemical Development) could not legally refuse entry to qualified women. It was through Osoaviakhim, a paramilitary organization, that most Soviet women received flight training.[27] Founded in 1927 to train teenagers and young adults in quasi-military skills such as defense and chemical warfare, marksmanship, and parachuting, by the 1930s it began developing a network of air clubs to provide flight training in light aircraft.[28]

The Soviet government emphasized the importance of aviation and air travel, which was seen as the most promising means of transportation, especially since the vast expanses of Soviet territory were still not linked by roads or railroads. Officially, young Soviet women were encouraged to participate in all facets of Osoaviakhim training. However, many women encountered obstacles when attempting to get into flight training. Marina Chechneva (who subsequently became a night bomber pilot and a Hero of the Soviet Union in World War II) described the manner in which her male flying club instructor discouraged her from seeking a career as a pilot as being typical of the time:

Quite a few women were studying at the air club; however, the attitude of many of the instructors towards them was, to put it mildly, less than enthusiastic. The instructors took women in their groups unwillingly. That was clear. Women were only beginning to enter aviation. Not everyone believed that we would be able to work in this field on an equal basis with men. The example of famous women pilots did not convince the skeptics. "Aviation is not a woman's affair" they declared repeatedly, and tried in every way possible to dissuade young women from joining the air club.[29]

Nevertheless, many Soviet women persevered and learned to fly. By 1941, 100–150 air clubs had been established; one out of every three or four pilots was a woman.[30] Even when their instructors were supportive, some of the young women faced opposition from their parents. Anna Bondareva, later a Guards lieutenant and navigator in the 46th Regiment, related the following story:

> When I was in the seventh grade, an airplane came to our town. In 1936 it seemed something extraordinary. A campaign was launched spontaneously: "Young Boys and Girls, Take Up Aviation!" Being a Komsomol member, I was, of course, in the front ranks and immediately joined an air club. Father was dead against it, though. Until then all the members of my family had been steelworkers, with several generations of blast-furnace operators. My father believed that a woman could be a steelworker but never a pilot.[31]

It is interesting that the idea of women flying airplanes was more foreign to Russian men in the 1930s than the concept of female steelworkers. In the United States at that time, possibly the opposite was true. This perception may be because of the fact that there were more women steelworkers employed in the USSR than there were women aviators. In light of this, women faced many hurdles in becoming pilots before the war, despite the Soviet decree that guaranteed gender equality. The purpose of the pilot training (for the men anyway) in the Osoaviakhim was to prepare them for either active or reserve military duty. The men who received flight training at the air clubs were registered in the military reserve forces, but women were not. No provisions were made for women pilots to play a military role until the German invasion in June 1941.

The women pilots and navigators who were recruited soon after the invasion for Marina Raskova's 122nd Composite Air Group (that later became the 586th Fighter Aviation Regiment, the 587th Day Bomber Aviation Regiment, and the 588th Night Bomber Aviation Regiment) were subjected to a rigorous training program, and in the case of the pilots, one that crammed nearly three years of flying experience into several months. The women's instruction, equipment, and ultimate assignment were identical to those of their male counterparts. A significant proportion of the ground crews attached to the regiments were women as well. Responsible for maintaining and preparing the aircraft for their oftentimes numerous daily missions, the armorers and mechanics handled ammunition boxes and machine-gun belts, made quick-time repairs, and attached heavy bombs, often working without cover in subzero weather. The ground crews were as dedicated as the aircrew, and they grew close to their pilots and aircraft.[32]

Although the majority of the women recruited for the aviation regiments were young and single, some were married and some had children. Many of the married women had lost husbands or children in the war. Dusia Nosal, who became the first woman aviator to be awarded the Hero of the Soviet Union during the war, lost her baby in the bombing at the beginning of the war and was later killed in action herself. Other mothers left their children with relatives. Raskova had an eight-year-old daughter named Tanya whom she left with her mother. Aircraft mechanic Inna V. Pasportnikova, in an interview with historian Pennington, recalled, "The main complication was with women with children. There had to be someone to take care of the children."[33]

While Raskova set to work to form the women's air regiments, the Germans were advancing closer and closer to Moscow. Soviet citizens learned from radio reports that Moscow was in imminent danger of occupation. It was imperative that the women pilots be trained quickly so that they could participate in aerial combat in defense of their country. Raskova personally interviewed every volunteer. Most all of the women wanted to be utilized as pilots, but navigators were badly needed too, and Raskova chose those pilots with a technical education to fill the navigator slots. A minimum of 500 flying hours was required of women who desired to serve as fighter or bomber pilots. Uniforms were issued, but as there were no women's uniforms, the recruits were forced to wear the oversized flight suits of male airmen, similar to the clothing given to the WASP. Pants could be hitched up with belts and the cuffs could be rolled up, but footwear was a problem. If the oversized uniforms made them look ridiculous, the men's boots made the women look clumsy. Pilot Raisa E. Aronova recalled: "They gave us men's clothing, right down to the underwear."[34]

The day after the women were given their uniforms, Raskova received orders to send the aviation group immediately to Engels, a city on the Volga River north of Stalingrad, to complete the formation and training there. In Moscow there was panic among its citizens as the Germans drew closer. During the night of 16–17 October 1941 when the women departed for Engels, 100 trains carrying 150,000 people reportedly left Moscow.[35]

These first trainees, who numbered between 300 and 400, were greeted by exceptionally cold weather (four degrees below zero Fahrenheit) after spending nine days on the train. The girls passed the time on the long journey studying military regulations, singing, and tailoring their uniforms. Food was scarce, and there was no possibility of bathing while on the train. Raskova, who spent time in each of the cars during the trip to Engels, advised the trainees that they should sleep as much as they could. Aronova recalled Raskova telling them to "rest, because ahead lie very demanding studies."[36]

Once in Engels, the first order that was issued was for all the girls to get a "boy-style" haircut. Night bomber pilot Nadezhda Popova recalled the order. "I remember one girl with gorgeous long hair crying, saying, 'Long hair is a woman's treasure, her beauty.' It was our first taste of military discipline."[37] According to Shelley Saywell in her book *Women in War,* in an ironic twist, an air force general, arriving to inspect the women weeks later, lifted one woman's cap off, and the long hair she had refused to cut off came tumbling down. There was silence on the parade ground. Then he said, "Now that is what a woman should look like. Why do all of you want to look like boys?"[38] When they got to the front, most of the women grew their hair back.

Studies began in earnest. During the next few months, the members of the 122nd Group underwent an extremely condensed, intensive course of training. There were ten courses a day plus two hours of drill; navigators studied Morse code for an additional hour and rose earlier than the other students, who slept on average five or six hours a night.[39] To prepare the trainees for the difficult conditions at the front, Raskova would sometimes sound an alarm in the middle of the night, requiring everyone to dress and form up outdoors by putting on their overcoats over their nightshirts, making them march around the airfield with the cold wind blowing on their bare legs.[40] For many of the women who were barely out of their teens, military life was a difficult adjustment. Some of the girls had never been away from home before. Conditions were poor at the front, and the women were forced to cope with an entirely new way of life. One woman told Saywell many years after the war:

> But your evaluation of things changed. What seemed absolutely horrible in the beginning gradually became more or less acceptable. Later, when new women arrived at the front and experienced the hardships for the first time, we would wonder what they were upset about. We were used to not washing for weeks, to the lack of privacy, to the embarrassment of lice inspections. Under fire for the first time new recruits would be hysterical, while we had become calm about it.[41]

Raskova, then thirty years old, oversaw all aspects of the women's combat training. She drove herself hard and was sometimes so exhausted that she did not have the strength to undress at night and slept on top of her bed in her uniform. To her trainees, she encompassed immeasurable energy and endurance. Ekaterina Fedotova, later a flight commander in the 125th Regiment, remembered a time when she had gone into Raskova's office and found her asleep on her table. When she tried to leave without disturbing her, Raskova opened her eyes and, without moving, said, "Give your report. I'm listening."[42] A talented musician, Raskova would sometimes sneak away from her work late at night to play the piano, which would help to calm her nerves. Respected and loved by the women she trained, she was soft-spoken and friendly with a keen sense of humor and a kind heart.

"When we were in training we would sit in our dug-out around the stove and she [Raskova] would sing to us," said Valentina Kravchenko, a navigator in the 587th Day Bomber Aviation Regiment. "She'd say, 'Girls, when the war is over'...and she'd look at us in our unattractive flying suits that made us look like bears...'After the war you'll wear white dresses and pretty shoes, and we'll have a big party. Don't worry; we're going to win the war.'"[43]

Tragically, Raskova did not live to see the end of the war. While in the process of transferring her regiment to the front at Stalingrad on January 4, 1943, the plane Raskova was piloting crashed after being caught in a heavy snowstorm and dense fog, killing all four crew members aboard. Raskova, who had been commander of the 125th Regiment for only a few months, never got to experience combat herself.

Raskova's death came as a great shock to her fellow pilots and countrymen. Her regiment pledged to become worthy of bearing Raskova's name when the honorary title of Guards was conferred on it on September 23, 1943.[44] Pilot Ekaterina Riabova, squadron commander of the 588th Night Bomber Aviation Regiment, in a letter home to her family wrote: "I will always remember her young, beautiful, brave, her face looking tired and intense." [45] For navigator Galina Brok-Beltsova, Raskova was a powerful role model to her young pilots. "For inspiration we had a portrait of Raskova at our base, and we each carried a picture of her in a pocket on the leg of our flight suits," she said. "The pocket had a clear covering over it, so we could see her picture. We all called ourselves, 'Raskovsi,' belonging to Raskova. She was brave, and so we were brave."[46]

Raskova was posthumously awarded the Order of the Patriotic War, First Class, and her ashes were interned in the Kremlin Wall beside those of Osipenko. Raskova had been acutely aware that she and her fellow female flyers were making history. In May 1942, she had told the members of the 588th Regiment after accompanying them to the front near Stavropol: "I believe that all of you will come back as heroes. Epics and songs will be composed about you. You will be glorified by future generations."[47]

In early 1942 when the three air regiments were formed under the auspices of the 122nd Group, by late spring the women received orders to go to the front. On the morning of May 23, 1942, garrison commander Colonel Bagaev made a short speech to the crews of the 588th Regiment who soon would be experiencing their first taste of combat:

Today, for the first time, a woman's regiment leaves our airfield for the front. You do not fly on awesome machines, but on training aircraft. And it's true that you yourselves are not excessively awesome in appearance. But I am certain that in these light-winged airplanes, you will be able to inflict heavy blows on your enemy. Let fly with you my fatherly wish: success to you and combat glory![48]

The women flyers were anxious to test their training in action, and no pilot could forget her first encounter with the enemy. Nadezhda Popova, assigned to the 588th Night Bomber Aviation Regiment, recalled her first combat mission near the southern front in the Ukraine:

> It was a very, very dark night. Not one small star could be seen. The sky was covered in cloud; it seemed that it was an abyss of darkness, pitch black...and when I got up in the air, I could see the front line marked by green, red and white tracer lights, where skirmishes continued throughout the night. I followed the lights towards the accumulation of enemy troops. Suddenly, the plane in front of mine got caught in three and later five projector lights, which blind pilots. I watched them fall to the earth right in front of my eyes and saw the explosion of flames below. I flew towards the enemy lines, thinking I must help my friends. Irrational thoughts...I knew they were dead. We dropped the bombs on the dots of light below. They shot at us and I circled round and flew back towards the base. When I landed I could see they already knew. I was ordered to fly another mission immediately. It was the best thing to keep me from thinking about it.[49]

"The stress was huge," said Irina Rakobolskaya, chief of staff of the 588th Night Bomber Aviation Regiment.

> We were keen to show we could fight as well as, if not better than the men. When they first saw us, they didn't take us seriously. They called us silly girls who should still be playing with dolls. They didn't believe we could fly. They were very derogatory. But in six months, their attitude changed completely. In 1943 our regiment was the first in the division to be awarded the honor of becoming a Guards regiment.[50]

One of the best-known Soviet woman pilots in the war, who became famous for being a double ace, was Lidiya (nicknamed "Lilya") Litvyak. A senior lieutenant as well as a flight commander of the 73rd Guards *Stalingrad-Vienna* Fighter Regiment/6th Fighter Division/8th Air Army, she also served in the 586th as well as two other fighter regiments. Born August 18, 1921, in Moscow, Litvyak, learned to fly at a young age. It is fitting that her birthday falls on Air Fleet Day—the day Russia honors its air forces. Striking in appearance and small in stature, she made a powerful impression on everyone who came in contact with her. A lover of nature, she is said to have decorated the inside of her cockpit with wildflowers found near the airfield, and legend has it that she painted a white lily on the fuselage of her aircraft. No one could have predicted that this petite blonde pilot (she had to have the pedals of her plane adjusted so she could reach them), who liked to fashion colorful neck scarves out of parachutes, would prove to be such a deadly adversary in the skies.

On September 13, 1942, Litvyak would go down in history as the first woman in the world to shoot down an enemy aircraft. She downed two German fighters that day in an intense air battle over Stalingrad that involved a German ace named Erwin Maier who was a three-time recipient of the Iron Cross. He had scored his eleventh victory three days earlier. Maier was forced to bail out of his aircraft, and once captured on the ground, he asked to meet the Russian ace who had shot down his plane. When the twenty-one-year-old Litvyak stood before him he stared in amazement. In disbelief he demanded proof that she had indeed been the pilot he had fought with. After Litvyak described in detail their dogfight (which had been her first), Maier was forced to believe her account. According to an article by Vladimir Belyakov, when Maier had accepted the bitter truth, he knelt down beside her and ceremoniously offered her his Swiss-made gold watch—a great luxury in Russia at that time. Litvyak's response to the gesture was to say, "I do not accept gifts from my enemies," after which she abruptly turned and walked away.[51] For a pilot of her limited experience to achieve two kills in a single day (especially one involving a fighter ace) was an amazing accomplishment.

After having been wounded on several occasions, Litvyak was reportedly shot down near the town of Krasny Luch in the Luhansk region, Ukraine on August 1, 1943, in an air battle that approximately nine Soviet and forty enemy aircraft took part in. It was not until 1979 that the remains of a woman believed to be that of Litvyak were discovered near the Ukrainian village of Dmitreivka. Her body was said to be found buried under the wing of a Yak-1. Because DNA testing was not available at the time, it has not been proven conclusively that the body of the female pilot recovered is actually that of Litvyak.

In 2004, Ekaterina K. Polunina, a senior aircraft mechanic with the 586th Fighter Regiment and the unit's historian and archivist, published a book in Russia that raises new questions about the fate of Litvyak. In light of new archival evidence, Polunina now believes that Litvyak may have survived the crash, been taken prisoner by the Germans, and possibly escaped from the Soviet Union after the war. According to Polunina, someone saw a woman fighter pilot matching Litvyak's description being led away by the German military after she landed in the Ukraine. She tells of the Soviet air force command post hearing Litvyak's voice on German radio, and Soviet fighter pilot Vladimir Lavrinenko seeing her in the POW camp where he says they were both incarcerated.[52]

Because of her missing-in-action status, Litvyak was not awarded the Gold Star of Hero of the Soviet Union until May 5, 1990, when Mikhail Gorbachev signed the decree, forty-seven years following her presumed death. Litvyak's younger brother Yuri Kunavin accepted the medal on her behalf. Having flown 268 combat sorties in less than two years, Litvyak is believed to have shot down twelve enemy planes and also had three shared kills to her credit. Polunina, however, after analyzing the regimental documents, believes that Litvyak's victories were exaggerated and that proper credit should be given to Ekaterina ("Katya") V. Budanova, Litvyak's friend and fellow fighter pilot.[53] According to Polunina, the corrected score should stand at five autonomous and two group victories (including an artillery observation balloon) for Litvyak and six independent and four group victories for Budanova, who was killed on July 19, 1943, in a battle with three Messerschmitts. To this day, Litvyak and Budanova remain the world's top-rated women fighter aces. A male air crewman who knew Litvyak during the war described her as "a remarkable girl, smart, with the true character of a fighter pilot and a daredevil."[54]

The young Soviet women flyers were fueled with intense feelings of patriotism and a deep desire to do something to help their countrymen and women defeat the Nazis who were occupying their land. Like the American WASP, they sought the opportunity to serve their country in its hour of need. The Russian women were in a unique position, however, to inflict direct blows to the enemy, and downing a German aircraft became retribution for the lost lives of their friends and fallen comrades. Despite the women pilots' proven heroism, the USSR soon forgot their wartime contributions. In 1945, Soviet society encouraged women who had fought at the front to discard their uniforms and return home to reestablish their prewar roles as housewives and mothers. After World War II, Soviet aviation remained off limits to women. It would be several decades before female pilots were given the opportunity to fly military aircraft again.

CHAPTER 3

Patriotism and a Love of Flying

I've been waiting on the flight line, just for a chance to fly
I've been waiting on the flight line, for an hour in the sky
Can't you hear the props a-roaring, warming up the line
Can't you hear the ships a-calling, come Fifinella, fly.

—WASP Song[1]

When America went to war in December 1941 following the attack on Pearl Harbor, the country solicited the involvement of women in all aspects of war production and encouraged their enlistment as volunteers in the armed forces. Although American women served in similar auxiliaries in World War I, they were recruited in record numbers three decades later. The largest number of women joined the female corps of the military branches: 140,000 served with the Women's Army Auxiliary Corps [in 1943 the organization dropped the "Auxiliary" and became the WAC (Women's Army Corps)]; 100,000 with the Navy's Women Accepted for Voluntary Emergency Service; 23,000 with the Marine Corps Women's Reserve; 13,000 with the Coast Guard's Semper Paratus Always Ready; and a little over 1,000 women served as WASP.[2]

For the women in the Soviet Union, this was not the first time they had been called for duty by their country. According to an article by Dale R. Herspring, approximately 5,000 women fought in World War I.[3] The most well-known of these women warriors were the all-female Battalion of Death formed by Mariya Bochkareva in 1917, who tried unsuccessfully to defend the Winter Palace during the October Revolution. Unlike women recruited for service in women's auxiliaries in other nations, including the United States, the Russian women soldiers were armed and trained for combat.

Bochkareva's call for women to volunteer as soldiers emphasized feminine values. "We women are turning into tigresses to protect our children from a shameful yoke to protect the freedom of our country," she told her recruits.[4] Bochkareva explained that maternal instinct, not a quest for glory or adventure, was what sent the women into the trenches. A significant part of their mission was, by their example, to shame soldiers in the Imperial Russian Army into fighting. Although the women's Battalion of Death was short-lived, the Russian Civil War that followed saw women fighting on every front. The Great Patriotic War would continue women's presence on the battlefields of Russia.

Russian women pilots were also utilized in World War I, though to a lesser degree. Eugenie Shakhovskaya, a princess born in St. Petersburg in 1889, was hailed as the world's "first military airwoman"[5] when she flew as an aerial reconnaissance pilot for the Russian Imperial Army. Another woman aviator who flew as an air scout, Nadezhda Degtereva, reportedly disguised herself as a man and entered military service in 1914. It was not until she was wounded while flying over enemy lines on the Austrian front in Galicia that her true sex was discovered.[6] Princess Sophie Alexandrovna Dolgorukaya is also believed to have flown for the Russian Air Service in 1917 after Alexander Kerensky, the leader of the Provisional Government, opened military service to women.

In the United States, unlike the USSR, women's experiences taking up arms against an enemy was spotty at best. The government employed creative ways to attract the involvement of women in the war. Propaganda posters were produced by the OWI (Office of War Information) to lure American women out of the home and into the factories. In its push to recruit women, the United States government was careful to portray the woman war worker as unmistakably feminine. Some people feared that women would ultimately lose their femininity if they took on the jobs left by men. The reinforcement of women's traditional roles was also extended to the jobs depicted in the posters. The gap between a woman's domestic duties and her work duties was intentionally blurred by government policy, which suggested that women be told that war work was "pleasant and as easy as running a sewing machine, or using a vacuum machine."[7] The OWI recognized that the menial jobs would need to be associated with a noble cause in order for them to attract women. According to Maureen Honey in her book *Rosie the Riveter: Class, Gender, and Propaganda during World War II,* "These jobs will have to be glorified as patriotic war service if American women are to be persuaded to take them and stick to them."[8]

Women were also a popular subject of propaganda posters in the Soviet Union. Mother Russia was portrayed in one of the best-known recruiting posters as a "handsome, middle-aged woman in a billowing red peasant dress and scarf, her arms raised in a summoning gesture, her expression firm and admonitory. Over her head is emblazoned, also in red: 'The Motherland is calling!'"[9] The poster appealed to Soviet men's feelings of loyalty to their land as well as their women, and both were viewed to be in need of defending as the German invaders stormed through their country. For women, the poster honored their contribution to the war, and illustrated their vital role as maintainers of Soviet morale.

According to Lisa A. Kirschenbaum, "Mothers functioned in Soviet propaganda both as national symbols and as the constantly reworked and re-imagined nexus between home and nation, between love for the family and devotion to the state."[10] Kirschenbaum went on to point out that the Soviet insistence on both the vulnerability and the self-reliance of women paralleled that of the American female war worker. Propaganda in the United States urged the acceptance of women in male jobs, yet was also aimed at preserving their femininity.

During World War II, women most frequently enlisted in war work out of patriotism and a desire to promote victory. The American women who signed up for the female corps of the armed services were portrayed as being "just as feminine as before they enlisted." Colonel Oveta Culp Hobby, director of the WAC, sought to portray women's service in terms of their traditional feminine relationships and responsibilities, and she recommended advertising copy which pointed out that servicewomen would be hastening the return of their sweethearts and husbands by "only performing the duties women would ordinarily do in civilian life."[11]

According to WASP Anne Noggle, the overwhelming reason why women pilots were attracted to the WASP program was a desire to serve their country. Some had other reasons, she pointed out, like women who had "husbands, fiancés, sweethearts, fathers, or brothers in uniform."[12] Women who had loved ones serving overseas often sought solace in wartime work, hoping that their contributions would help to bring their men home sooner. WASP Anne McClellan's pilot husband had been missing since the Baatan Death March, and Ah Ying ("Hazel") Lee, an American of Chinese ancestry, was engaged to (and later married) a major in the Chinese Air Force. Some of the women, like twenty-two-year-old Rebecca Edwards, were already widows of the war. In the book she published on her experiences as a WASP, Noggle wrote, "No doubt the women loved to fly as much as the male pilots, and some were accused of joining to seek 'affairs of the heart.' But over and above all other reasons was the feeling that they were making a direct and useful contribution—that they were able to do something for the war effort."[13]

Cornelia Fort, one of the first WAFS pilots, wrote a moving account of her reasons for becoming a wartime pilot in *Woman's Home Companion* in July 1943. The article was published posthumously after she became the first woman pilot to die on war duty in American history, when the bomber she was piloting crashed in Texas on March 21, 1943. In the article, twenty-four-year-old Fort emphasized the important role the women pilots were performing in the war: "We have no hopes of replacing men pilots. But we can each release a man to combat, to faster ships, to overseas work. Delivering a trainer to Texas may be as important as delivering a bomber to Africa if you take the long view. We are beginning to prove that women can be trusted to deliver airplanes safely and in the doing serve the country which is our country too."[14]

The native of Tennessee, who had been giving a flying lesson over Pearl Harbor on the morning it was attacked by the Japanese, witnessed firsthand the devastation of the aerial invasion. The harrowing experience only fueled her determination to fly for her country. In the article she went on to write:

> As long as our planes fly overhead the skies of America are free and that's what all of us everywhere are fighting for. And that we, in a very small way, are being allowed to help keep that sky free is the most beautiful thing I have ever known. I, for one, am profoundly grateful that my one talent, my only knowledge, flying, happens to be of use to my country when it is needed. That's all the luck I ever hope to have.[15]

WASP Doris Brinker Tanner acknowledged the unique wartime role played by her fellow female flyers. "We women pilots viewed America from a perspective then shared by few other groups—and we deeply, sincerely loved our country."[16] In her book *Winning My Wings: A Woman Airforce Service Pilot in World War II,* Marion Stegeman Hodgson commented on the historical significance of what the WASP were doing in the war: "We were just grateful to have a chance to do something women had never before been allowed to do in our country: fly military airplanes."[17] In a radio interview on National Public Radio, Libby Gardiner, who flew the B-26 during the war as a WASP, echoed Hodgson's sentiment: "We just felt we had really won a prize to get to fly these airplanes, which were off limits for us in any ordinary way, and to get paid for doing it and to know that we were contributing to the war effort—it was just too much. Very few men ever got a chance like that and here we were getting this chance."[18] Motivated by patriotism, a love of flying, and a keen sense of adventure, the pilots, like many American women, sought to contribute their special talents to help win the war. A WASP motto helps to illustrate this feeling experienced by the airwomen:

> To serve; to add my strength to theirs
> Who give their all;
> To fly; to do my part
> Is all I ask.[19]

In addition to the strong feelings of patriotism that drew the female pilots to the war, the women's strong personalities as well as their yearning for adventure, attributed to their decision to join the WASP program. Ann Baumgartner Carl, later became the first woman to fly a jet, had graduated from Smith College and was looking for new challenges when she learned of the women pilot training program in Texas. "I had done a lot of other adventurous things—mountain climbing and training horses and things like that, and it just seemed like the next step,"[20] she said in *Fly Girls*, a documentary film on the WASP. The flying bug bit Carl hard after only her first lesson. She recalled the moment in her book *A WASP Among Eagles: A Woman Military Test Pilot in World War II:* "When I got home, the light of the sky continued to fill my mind. I could still feel us drifting above the treetops. I could not sit still. I circled round and round the room, imagining dangerous wartime rescues, flying on and on above the land and the clouds. I felt suddenly more alive. This is what I was made for, I told myself."[21]

Carl's interest in aviation could have also been awakened early on by a visit to her school by Amelia Earhart after the famous flyer's historic flight in 1932. Carl was seated in the front row. Once she earned her pilot's license and had acquired the necessary flight hours, the expectation of adventure convinced Carl to leave her job as a writer for *The New York Times*, in order to train alongside her fellow women pilots, who would be given the unprecedented opportunity to fly military aircraft in wartime America. "I thought of all the things I had been interested in as I grew up," Carl wrote in her book. "And they all seemed to have the aura of adventure. Now there was the added impetus to become part of the war effort, in some way."[22] Incidentally, Carl would be the only woman jet pilot in America for almost a decade—until Jacqueline Cochran broke the sound barrier in 1953. The first man to fly faster than the speed of sound was Chuck Yeager who broke the sound barrier flying the experimental Bell X-1 at Mach 1 at an altitude of 45,000 feet on October 14, 1947.

Jean Hascall Cole, who joined the WASP trainees in Sweetwater, Texas in 1943, marveled at the motley band of women who converged on the dusty little town to become the first military pilots in the history of the United States. In her book on the WASP Cole wrote: "As I was to learn, we came from all corners of America, from the small towns and the big cities, from the privileged classes and the not-so-privileged. For each of us, flying was a passion, and some combination of daring, rebellion, and determination took us into the air."[23] Despite the varied backgrounds and lives of the WASP, each of the women pilots shared a fierce resolve to succeed and a desire to volunteer their services for the betterment of their country.

In the Soviet Union, like the United States, the women pilots were not drafted into military service as the men were; they volunteered to serve in the air force. In Russia, women fought to defend their beloved motherland that was being ravished by German forces. According to Reina Pennington,

"It would be difficult to overstress patriotism as a motivation"[24] for the women's active involvement in the war. Pennington points out that the Soviet women pilots did not simply support their nation in its time of need; they were willing to kill to do it. They fought for the right to fight, insisting on using their special skills in aviation.

The Soviet women pilots not only faced the test of combat but, like the WASP, also had to continually prove themselves to their own country. The women were acutely aware that they had to meet or even surpass the standards set by male aviators. Navigator Polina Gelman noted, "We were always trying to prove that we were as good as men. This of course was one of the incentives."[25] The women could not fail to recognize that many men questioned their abilities, and they were constantly being judged and tested.

Although many of the young Soviet women pilots volunteered as a result of an initial overwhelming surge of patriotism, they quickly came to realize that the war was nothing short of a national life-or-death struggle. A number of women pilots, however, had other motivations for joining the air force and becoming military flyers besides patriotism. Fighter ace Lidiya Litvyak hoped that by proving herself to be a competent and brave fighter pilot, she could redeem her family name. Her father had been among the thousands imprisoned and killed in 1937 for charges that were never made clear. Litvyak never doubted her father's innocence, and she believed that her fame in combat could erase his status as an enemy of the people. Litvyak's deepest fear, according to her aircraft mechanic Inna V. Pasportnikova, was becoming missing in action. In the Soviet Union any soldier whose body could not be found, that is, who went "missing without a trace," were automatically suspected of desertion. Sadly, Litvyak herself would go missing in action when she was shot down on August 1, 1943, during an air battle. The body of a young woman, believed by some to be Litvyak, was discovered thirty-six years later in a common grave.

Fighter pilot Katya Budanova, who died in the war, wrote a letter home to her sister explaining her participation in the conflict:

> Olechka, my darling...I am now devoting my entire life to the struggle against the vile Nazi creatures. I would like to tell you this: I am not afraid to die, but I don't want to die...If I am fated to perish, my death will cost the enemy dearly. My dear winged "Yak" is a good machine and our lives are inseparably bound up together; if the need arises, we shall both die like heroes. Keep well, my dear, love the Homeland more, and work even harder than before for its benefit. Love and kisses. Katya.[26]

The women's decision to fight to the death on behalf of their country was also provoked by tragedies that struck close to home. After her brother was killed in the early days of the war, Nadezhda Popova promised to avenge his death and sent a cable to Moscow asking to be sent to the front to fight. Witnessing firsthand the death and destruction caused by the Germans in her town, Popova wanted to do what she could to rid the invaders from her country. "When the German planes flew over us we could see the smiling faces of the Nazi pilots while they shot into the crowds, gunning down the women and children fleeing to the east with their bicycles, cribs, bundles on their backs," she remembered. "I couldn't believe what I was seeing."[27] During the war, Popova's family home became a Gestapo police station, where Soviet citizens were tortured. "It was like a terrible storm had invaded our country," she said. "The war changed our lives forever."[28]

The Soviet women pilots who volunteered for combat service were individuals who shared an adventurous spirit and who were not afraid to stray from the traditional views held of women during that time. Something inside of them yearned to explore and to be free, and this sensation often led them to aviation. Popova, who was one of the first women pilots to join Raskova's regiments, learned to parachute when she was a teenager. "I was a very lively, energetic, wild kind of person. I loved to tango, foxtrot, but I was bored. I wanted something different. Most of the girls I knew didn't want to learn to fly. They were frightened, especially of jumping. I don't know why, but it never frightened me."[29]

Like the WASP, many of the Soviet women flyers dreamed from a very young age of becoming pilots. The possibility of flying high above the clouds was often a welcome escape from their humdrum existences in small towns. Some women lived near airports or had an opportunity to see airplanes up close when an air show came to their city. The destiny of famous pilot Polina Osipenko, who accompanied Raskova on the historic *Rodina* flight in 1938, was changed forever in 1930 when two sport aircraft landed in a field on the outskirts of her village. Along with the rest of her town, she went to take a look at the airplane, an unusual sight in her village located on the shore of the Azov Sea. She spoke with the pilots, one of whom happened to be a woman. The experience made a strong impression on the twenty-three-year-old, and Osipenko was soon making inquiries about admission to flying schools.[30] Yevgeniya Zhigulenko, who later became a flight commander for the 46th Guards Aviation Regiment, exhibited an early love for adventure and outdoor sports as a youth, developing a passion for parachute jumping. After learning of the flights of famous airwomen Valentina Grizodubova, Polina Osipenko, and Marina Raskova on the radio, Zhigulenko decided that her future lay in aviation. Four decades later in 1981, Zhigulenko produced and directed the Russian film *The Night Witches in the Sky,* based on her flying experiences in the war.

Witnessing firsthand the scourge of fascism at their doorstep, the Soviet airwomen answered the call to defend their Motherland in a way that would have a quantitative impact on the war. As thousands of their countrymen and women were forced to submit to German forces, the female flyers avenged their deaths in the skies above the Eastern Front. Unlike the WASP, who had a noncombat role in the war, their Russian counterparts were in a unique position to render death to the enemy. The young women, mostly in their late teens and early twenties, fought not only for the preservation of their homeland but also for their place in it. Combining an adventurous spirit and a forceful determination, the women pilots of both nations were resolved not only to help bring about an Allied victory but also to prove to their countries that they could be counted on to perform their duty in one of modern history's greatest conflicts.

CHAPTER 4

Gender Issues

I guess there was some [sexism] honey, but I'll tell you I wanted the flying so bad that I wasn't going to let anything stop me. As far as I was
concerned, it was "all the luck I ever hoped to have."
—WASP Phyllis Tobias Felker (44-W-2)[1]

The American and the Russian women pilots were well aware that they
would be continuously tested and scrutinized by the male pilots and aircrews they worked with on the air bases. Most men were not comfortable
with the idea of female pilots, and many flatly refused to fly in an airplane
piloted by a woman. Flying—especially military flying—was primarily a
man's domain at the time, and the airwomen endured discrimination and
sexism even as they successfully flew military aircraft. In the end, female
pilots of both nations earned the respect of male aircrews. It took, however,
the hard work and dedication of the women flyers to overcome the prejudices against them. The excellent flight record of the WASP and Soviet women
pilots proved, not only to their male counterparts, but also to the world, that
women had successfully passed the test. The pilots' contributions helped to
overcome the doubts of many cynics who did not see any value in utilizing
women aviators in the war.

Gender was the defining factor of the WASP program. Women accepted
into WASP training had to be proven flyers with pilot licenses and seventy-
five hours of flight time (later reduced to thirty-five), while male trainees
did not have to have pilot licenses or any flight experience whatsoever to
join the USAAF's pilot training program. The Army Air Forces also treated
the administration of the WASP program differently. The details of the
women pilots' training program remained a closely guarded secret, and

since the WASP's public relations plan discouraged media contact, the public and Congress knew little of their accomplishments during the war. America's limited knowledge of the women pilots and their successful wartime missions was an important factor in the WASP's failed attempt to militarize in 1944.

According to Byrd Howell Granger, who graduated in the first WASP class, the women's flying program was experimental and that placed additional pressure on the women to prove that their gender was not a detriment to flying. "Could women fly?" she said. "Well, as for me, I've never gotten into an aircraft yet that has asked me what sex I was. If you knew how to fly—you flew. It was as simple as that."[2]

Although the women pilots were confident in their flying abilities, they recognized that their gender would be challenged in ways that could be both humiliating and invasive. In March 1943, the ATC ordered its women pilots grounded for the week they were menstruating. The 1942 CAA's *Handbook for Medical Examiners,* which directed the doctors who conducted physicals required for a student pilot to solo, stated: "A history should be obtained of any menstrual abnormalities, pregnancies and miscarriages. All women should be cautioned that it is dangerous for them to fly within a period of three days prior to and three days after the menstrual period."[3] In a matter of weeks, it became evident that the ferrying division was not going to enforce it. None of the men in high command were particularly anxious to monitor women pilots in this way, so the regulation was formally dropped. Whatever fears the ATC may have had about the dangers of women flying while menstruating proved unfounded. The WAFS had flown almost daily from December through March without a single accident, not even a minor mishap.[4]

In an interview, Jean Terrell Moreo McCreery, who graduated in the last WASP class of 44-W-10, laughed at the story of a military doctor's warning that the women might never be able to give birth to children because of their flying. "I have ten children," she said, "twenty-three grandchildren and three great-grandchildren."[5] Not surprising, no WASP ever reported having any trouble conceiving after the war because of their years of flying.

By the time the WASP graduated and were sent to their respective air bases for duty, they quickly became accustomed to the dumbfounded and unbelieving reactions they received from male pilots and air personnel. As the following story, recounted by WASP Carole Fillmore illustrates, many people were not even aware of the women pilots' existence. The women's presence in the air oftentimes took the men in the control tower completely by surprise.

On her way to Newark to deliver a P-51 Mustang, Fillmore flew from Long Beach to Athens, Georgia, where she ran out of daylight. She tuned in the Athens tower and called for landing instructions, but no one answered. She called the tower again but still no response. In minutes she was directly over the field. She began to circle, and asked for a radio check. Suddenly an exasperated voice could be heard in her earphones: "Will the woman who is calling please stay off the air, we're trying to bring in a P-51." Fillmore looked around in the growing dusk for the other Mustang. Seeing none, she called in again for landing clearance. "Will the lady who's trying to get in, please stay off the air!" shouted the tower. "We are trying to make contact with the P-51!" Fillmore was beginning to feel weary from her long day in the air, and her patience was running out. Finally, she pressed the button on the stick activating her throat mike. "For your information, the lady who is on the air is in the P-51," she said, and without waiting for an answer, turned on final approach and headed straight down the runway at 120 miles an hour. The radio suddenly came alive. "Yeah, man, I hear you, I hear you, did you see the light? You're coming in fine, just great." Fillmore made a perfect landing. "Aw, that was beautiful," the startled man in the tower called out.[6]

Sometimes the men's ignorance of the WASP resulted in hilarious encounters with the opposite sex, as Teresa James soon discovered after being transferred to Camp Davis in North Carolina, a mixed-gender air base. James was at the officers' club one night where a party was going on, and she found herself at a table with some P-47 pilots who were getting ready to go overseas:

> I was dancing with this guy and he was telling me all this air crap— blab, blab, blab—you know, the "I'm going away to war so can't we get together kind of thing"—the old story...and I said what kind of airplane is it? And he went on to beguile me—how it was a big engine and "do you know what could happen to me if the engine quit on take off?" The next morning in operations I'm in my flight suit writing up the manifest and that guy did a double take [when he saw me], I thought he was going to drop dead. After all these stories he was telling me about the P-47 and he had no idea I was a P-47 pilot.[7]

WASP were generally accepted by the young air force officers who were close to the women's own ages, but there were exceptions as Marion Stegeman Hodgson found out as soon as she arrived in Texas for training. In her account of her WASP years, she remembered the comments made by a particular male officer in Sweetwater, while waiting for the bus that would take her and her fellow trainees to Avenger Field. "While we milled around the lobby that morning, noisily waiting for our ride, two lieutenants strutted through the room pretending to ignore us as they wound their way toward the drugstore that adjoined the lobby. Just as they passed behind me, I heard one of them snort, 'More women pilots! I'd like to give a U to every damn one I ride with. I'm putting in for a transfer.'"[8]

The lieutenant was a check pilot, and the "U" he was referring to stood for "Unsatisfactory." If women pilots had proved themselves to USAAF leaders, men at lower levels of authority, especially the older male personnel, did not always accept them. WASP Katherine Landry recalled the hostile reception she received at an air base by a commander who had no tolerance for women flyers. "When we got to the tow target squadron at Biggs, the commanding officer was horrified. I guess he didn't know we were coming. He not only didn't want us to do anything for him, he didn't want to do anything for us. He wouldn't see about getting us proper quarters or anything."[9] According to Landry, the officer was eventually transferred to another base.

Given the fact that women were more the exception than the rule in military aviation during the war, air bases, especially the operations center, were not equipped with women's facilities. A WASP, after landing at an air base after a long day of flying, would find herself in the embarrassing position of asking a man to check if the "coast was clear" so she could use the men's bathroom. In an interview with the author, WASP Jean Downey Harman remembered such an experience: "In those days operations didn't have men's and women's restrooms. The sign said men's room, so I asked the guy if he would stand by for me while I went in and used it. He said, "Oh you're doing a man's job, you can go in there and be a man.""[10] Despite the harsh comment made to her, according to Harman, she and her fellow WASP generally shrugged off the men's rude remarks. "We just laughed at it—we thought it was terribly funny," she said.[11]

Incidentally, WASP did not have a "relief tube" to use inside their planes if they had to use the toilet while flying as the male pilots did. "You just had to control your bladder by not drinking too many liquids before a flight,"[12] recalled B. J. Williams. The women pilots hoped they could land and get to a bathroom fast enough. It proved more of a challenge on the cross-country trips.

Jo Wallace Orr got a little more than she bargained for when she delivered a B-25 to Dorval Field in Montreal as she described in an interview with the *Saturday Evening Post*. While checking in her aircraft, the clerk, busy checking papers, perfunctorily pushed a kit across the counter to her. Back at the hotel, Orr opened it and discovered condoms—something she confessed she had never seen before. On her next trip, Orr was once again handed the kit. This time she loudly cleared her throat and immediately got the attention of the very embarrassed soldier. "He just about died," she said.[13]

Orr was not alone in her embarrassing encounter with prophylactics. Most all of the WASP who wrote about their experiences after the war managed to recall at least one humorous tale that was unique to their gender. Marion Schorr Brown did not forget one particular winter ride to El Paso when she was flying with two male wingmen whom she was evaluating. In the winter months, according to Brown, the WASP wore men's long underwear to fly in. As they approached the southern states, the weather became warmer and it was customary for the women to discard layers of their clothing to keep cool. As Brown and her two wingmen approached the air base, she reached behind her to put her shirt on, and to her horror it was not there. Her plane had two cockpits, and it had apparently fallen into the second cockpit, which was impossible for her to access while she was in flight. Brown tried motioning to the two male pilots on either side of her to let her land before they did, but they did not understand her and were on the ground in no time, she recalled.

So I'm poking around out there and I think, what the heck am I going to do? And then I landed and right away they sent a jeep...follow me, you know? And the jeep would go that way and I would go the other way. And he's wondering what's the matter? She must be having problems. We had no radio communications so I take the farthest looking ramp I could find, taxi out that way. The jeep follows me thinking I got trouble. I have problems! So I get there and they're ready to jump up on the wing when I stop. When I opened the cockpit and canopy I held up a map in front of me and I said, just go away! I can taxi. I know how to get back to the ramp. "No ma'am, we'll help you," he said. So there was nothing I could do, he's up on the wing now. So I tell him, "will you get my shirt in the backseat and then go away for a minute?" I imagine they laughed about that one for a very long time.[14]

For many women pilots, gender was not something they believed needed to be overcome in order for them to gain respect in the field of aviation. It was no surprise that Jacqueline Cochran, who succeeded in setting up a profitable cosmetics company while at the same time setting world aviation records, took particular pleasure in her femininity. Cochran recalled later in her second autobiography:

I'm feminine but I can't say that I ever was a feminist. I remember when I crash-landed at Bucharest during that London race after hours of hard flying without having any food or water and being nearly chilled to the marrow with cold. I refused to get out of the plane until I had removed my flying suit and used my cosmetic kit. That was feminine and it was natural for me. It gave me the pick-up I needed and I wasn't ashamed to do it. I didn't want to be a man. I just wanted to fly. This doesn't mean that I'm not extremely proud of what women have been able to do in aviation. Women are just as capable as men in the air. Sometimes they are more capable, in fact. But I do believe that women, especially women like me, are many-sided creatures. As the poets might say, we're diamonds with many facets.[15]

Even though Cochran strictly forbade the WASP from dating male pilots, relationships nonetheless developed between the men and women, and after the war many of the WASP went on to marry flight instructors or male pilots with whom they had been stationed. It was not unusual for the airwomen to apply makeup and check their hair when making their approach to land at mixed-gender airfields. The WASP were serious pilots, but they were also young, spirited, and not above looking attractive to the opposite sex.

Florene Miller Watson, who was among the first WAFS, gained a reputation as an excellent navigator with a penchant for wanting to look her best. "Guys would want to follow me too, and I'd say, 'I don't care who follows me, but pay attention and don't you all be dumb and sit on your map and not know where you are," she recalled years later. Navigation was tricky business in those days with often only a compass, a map, and a watch. "Guys who knew me would say, 'When she gets her lipstick and comb out, you know we're getting close.' Guys kidded me a lot about that. I'd be bouncing all over the sky trying to get my hair done and my lipstick on and get myself organized for my landing."[16]

The clothing and makeup worn by the female pilots, as well as their general appearance, intrigued the public. Years earlier when Amelia Earhart ventured to capitalize on her fame by producing a line of sportswear, the press could not resist commenting. What the well-dressed male aviator might choose to wear never seemed to attract the attention of the media the same way as the women flyers' clothing.

The WASP were no exception, and the pilots received an extensive photo spread in *Life* magazine on July 19, 1943. The article acknowledged the young airwomen's patriotism and dedication. However, as Luanne C. Lea argued: "The *Life* article projects a female stereotype who is especially concerned with her appearance. [It] applies that the major problems in flight training are unattractive coveralls and varieties of headgear that will control but not disrupt hairdos as, 'feminine locks constantly creep into girl fliers' eyes.'"[17]

The article concludes opposite a full-page photograph of the WASP trainees sunbathing outside their barracks: "That flying agrees with them anyone can see as Uncle Sam's suntanned girl pilots march along at Avenger Field, lustily singing the Air Corps' 'Off we go into the wild blue yonder, climbing high into the sun!'"[18] This depiction of the WASP was consistent with the representation of women in the 1940s. In newsreels and magazine articles of the day, women were routinely referred to as "girls" or "gals." Even though men in uniform were sometimes called "boys," the reference to women as "gals" was often a subtle way to lower the status of women. Newspaper editors were convinced that the American public was more interested in learning about what women were wearing and how they looked, than what they were doing or saying.

In 1944, Hollywood released a movie entitled *Ladies Courageous* based on the WASP. Directed by John Rawlins, the black and white film starred Loretta Young, Geraldine Fitzgerald, and Diana Barrymore. Unfortunately for the female flyers, the movie capitalized on traditional and unflattering myths about women, instead of portraying the pilots as they really were. In his book *Heroes Without Legacy: American Airwomen, 1912–1944,* Dean Jaros described the way in which the WASP were represented in the film: "Hysterical outbursts in the face of danger, competition for the attention of men, foolish flying errors, and suicide attempts are the order of the day."[19] The real-life WASP distanced themselves as far away from the movie as they could. "It was horrible," Caro Bayley Bosca decided when she saw the movie at a theater near her base. "I was never so embarrassed in my life...everybody here knew it was rotten and sympathized with us."[20] Overcoming prejudices in their day-to-day flying jobs was challenging enough; they did not need any help from Hollywood. Unfortunately for the women pilots, however, the movie was released at the same time Congress was considering the WASP militarization bill in June 1944. The film's poor portrayal of the female flyers may have helped turn the congressmen against the WASP.

Across the Atlantic in Great Britain, women pilots in the ATA not only had to contend with the chauvinism from their male superiors but from their government as well. South African-born pilot Jackie Sorour Moggridge remembered how the existence of female ferrying pilots in the war was kept hush-hush. "The British government said they didn't want the Germans to know that they were so desperately in need of pilots that they had to call upon the women," she said. "If that's not a put down, ask me another."[21]

Moggridge confided later in an interview that a male bomber crew once smuggled her aboard their aircraft as they embarked on a bombing mission. "We were having supper and they suddenly said, 'why don't you come up with us—you can see what real fighting is like.' I was thrilled to bits. I wasn't scared at all," she remembered. "It was like a dream. It didn't feel real. I think it was like that for them too. They blocked out their minds from the fear. Of course I was told in the morning that I couldn't tell anyone [about the flight.]"[22]

In the beginning of the war, the Soviet women pilots experienced the same discrimination from their male colleagues as the WASP, despite the Soviet propaganda that advocated women's equality. With the intensity and innate hardships that came with fighting at the front, the Russian women pilots quickly earned the respect of the men they flew with, even those who questioned women's participation in the war and their ability to stand up to the pressures of combat. Olga Sholokhova, a pilot with the 125th Guards Aviation Regiment, remembered the enthusiastic reception she received by French male pilots when she was forced to make an emergency landing during a snowstorm in her Pe-2 dive bomber at their air base. As the Frenchmen

rushed to greet the pilot who had made a perfect landing in such poor vis-
ibility, they were shocked to find themselves face-to-face with Olga and
her copilot Valya Volkova. "And how surprised we were when we saw that
the pilots were two charming young girls," recalled the colonel of the air
squadron. "For the first time, we French pilots were able to speak on the
subject of flying with beautiful ladies in a time of war."[23] The French pilots
lavished praises on the Russian airwomen. "If we could pick all the flowers
in the world and lay them before your feet, we still would not be able to
express our delight to Soviet women pilots,"[24] they said. In 1960, a reunion
took place between the former pilots of the "Normandie-Niemen" Regiment and the women veterans in Moscow's House of Friendship. "Fraternal
greetings to my comrades-in-arms, young Soviet airwomen, who proved
themselves men's equals in valour while fighting against the common
enemy," read an inscription by French pilot Jacques André, who during
the war was awarded the title of Hero of the Soviet Union.[25]

The Russian women pilots shared pride in their wartime accomplishments. Not only were they pleased with their individual achievements in
combat, but they were also proud of their country which afforded them this
historic opportunity. Navigator Yevgeniya Guruleva-Smirnova recalled her
satisfaction in an interview with Anne Noggle in 1990:

> No other country in the world let women fly combat, but Stalin pro-
> claimed that our women could do everything, could withstand any-
> thing! It was a kind of propaganda to show that Soviet women were
> equal to men and could fulfill any task, to show how mighty and
> strong we were. Women could not only bring babies into being but
> could build hydroelectric plants, fly aircraft, and destroy the enemy.
> Even if Stalin hadn't let the girls fly we would have volunteered by
> the thousands for the army.[26]

According to Reina Pennington, available Soviet sources indicate little or
no difference in the numbers and types of missions flown by the women's
aviation regiments and other Soviet Air Force regiments. Chief of staff of
the 46th Guards Aviation Regiment Irina Rakobolskaya commented,
"Nobody made any allowances for our youth or sex. They demanded from
us nothing less than from a man's regiment."[27] Vladimir Lavrinenkov,
general-colonel of aviation during the war, confirmed that the women flew
the same types of missions and performed as well as the men:

> The women pilots served at the airfield on an equal footing with the
> men. And they even fought no worse than the men...It wasn't easy
> for the girls at the front. Especially the women fighter-pilots: air com-
> bat demanded from them unusual physical strength and endurance.
> And the fact that the girls without complaining bore all the difficulties

is a credit to them, and evoked tremendous respect from those around them.[28]

Major Valentin Markov, who replaced Marina Raskova upon her death as commander of the 587th Day Bomber Aviation Regiment in 1943, also stated that the women's regiments were treated the same as male regiments and given the same types of combat assignments. He admitted after the war, "There were times, though, when I wished the command would remember that they were women and not throw them into the inferno of fighting."[29] Markov had large shoes to fill when he was asked to replace the much beloved Raskova. Initially disliked by the women pilots who resented his strict discipline, they grew to admire him and the feelings became mutual.

> The women in my regiment were self-disciplined, careful, and obedient to orders; they respected the truth and fair treatment toward them. They never whimpered and never complained and were very courageous. If I compare my experience of commanding the male and female regiments, to some extent at the end of the war it was easier for me to command the female regiment. They had the strong spirit of a collective unit.[30]

There were some differences, however, in how male flight instructors treated their female students. Not accustomed to working with women, many of them had a difficult time adjusting. Instructor G. N. Meniailenko recalled that the men had trouble controlling their language in front of the women. When the male students would make a mistake, he said, "We swore at them on the ground and sometimes in the air as well. But it was forbidden to do anything like that while instructing the pilots of Marina Raskova's regiment. When it happened, they were offended and even cried...we had to rein ourselves in."[31]

The physical demands placed on the women were no different than the male pilots at the front, but the constant strain of nerves and lack of sleep took their toll on each of them. Some women developed temporary paralysis from the stress. Pilot Raisa Zhitova-Yushina lost the feeling in both her legs on her final combat mission in 1945 (she made 535 during the war) after experiencing paralysis many times because of this nerve problem. Many of the airwomen, especially mechanics, worried that the heavy work they had done in the war would make them incapable of bearing children. The mechanics, who rarely received the glory in battle as the pilots did, had an especially physically demanding job that did not take into consideration their gender. Senior mechanic Nina Karasyova-Buzina recalled the job she did in the war:

This work that we did was not really women's work, because of the weight of the bombs that we manually attached to the aircraft...the bombs weighed 25, 32, or 100 kilos each...some nights we lifted 3,000 kilos of bombs. Three of us lifted the bombs, working together. We did our work at night and were not allowed to have any light to work by. So we worked blind, fumbling in darkness for the proper place to attach the bombs...we worked in mud, frost, sleet, and water, and we were very precise in fixing the bombs. We had to work barehanded so that we could feel what we were doing.[32]

Sleeplessness was another problem that plagued the pilots, during as well as after, the war. Serafima Amosova-Taranenko remembered having to get by on only a few hours of sleep a day when she flew night missions in the 46th Guards Aviation Regiment:

After the war we had a lot of headaches, could not relax, and had very hard problems with our sleeping, because for nearly three years we turned over the day and night. During daytime we could sleep for only about four hours and that is not enough. Then, with training and briefing, there were a lot of sleepless nights. For the first year after the war everyone had problems with sleeping, and I know there were no sleeping pills. I couldn't sleep for at least three months.[33]

The airwomen were conscious of the particular dangers they faced being female pilots flying over enemy territory. If they were shot down and captured by the Germans, they presumed they would be tortured. Both pilots and navigators made a pact that if they were to find themselves in enemy territory they would shoot themselves in the head instead of risking capture. Many of the women feared imprisonment more than death. "I knew capture would mean rape and torture," remarked Nadezhda Popova in an interview. "That frightened me more than anything. We carried guns and knew if we were shot down over enemy territory to keep one bullet for ourselves."[34] Klavdia Deryabina also remembered the arrangement she had made with her copilot. "My co-pilot and I had agreed we'd never land on enemy territory," she said. "We decided better to crash the plane than be taken prisoner. A lot of us took that decision. You wouldn't want to be a 'Night Witch' in captivity. We'd have been doomed to torture."[35]

Perhaps in light of this decision, there were few Russian airwomen who fell into the hands of the Germans. Pilot Anna Timofeeva-Egorova was one of the few to survive her incarceration. On her 277th mission, Timofeeva-Egorova was shot down and captured by the enemy. After sustaining extensive injuries to her legs, back and head, as well as burns to her body, she was sent to the camps for five months before being liberated by Soviet troops in January 1945. It is not known if she was tortured by the Germans upon capture, but one can only imagine what a curiosity a Soviet woman pilot would be to the Germans who were not accustomed to seeing women engaged in aerial combat.[36]

For some of the women, the atrocities of war did not harden them but instead gave them a deeper appreciation for life. "Was the war a woman's business? Of course not," said Mariya Smirnova, a commander of the 46th Regiment. "There is an opinion about women in combat that a woman stops being a woman after bombing, destroying, and killing; that she becomes crude and tough," she said. "This is not true; we all remained kind, compassionate, and loving. We became even more womanly, more caring of our children, our parents, and the land that has nourished us."[37]

It was Popova's opinion that the women pilots' wartime missions transcended gender. Instead of the deaths and killings they experienced making them cold and unfeeling as many believed, she said she ultimately felt that it helped to make the women who shared in the experience, more understanding toward one another. She explained:

> I don't think you can separate men from women in this situation. War does not spare anyone; it doesn't distinguish between the sexes, or the young from the old. It was a who-will-win situation. They were destroying us and we were destroying them. There was no choice involved. That is the logic of war: it is the life or death, victory or be vanquished. I killed many men, but I stayed alive. I was bombing the enemy—the target—just some lights on the earth below. War requires the ability to kill, among other skills. But I don't think you should equate killing with cruelty. I think the risks we took and the sacrifices we made for each other made us kinder rather than cruel.[38]

It is interesting to note that after the war, despite their impressive record in aerial combat, the majority of women veterans interviewed said they did not think women should participate in combat. It was clear that the women were proud of their achievements, but they believed women should only serve in combat if their country was threatened by a national emergency as it was in the Great Patriotic War. Many veterans also questioned their countrywomen who wished to fly military aircraft in peacetime. It was not that the women were adopting an antifeminist stance necessarily but instead were reflecting the traditionalist views they had always held. Navigator Alexandra Akimova explained in Noggle's book why she believed combat was against a woman's nature:

> The very nature of a woman rejects the idea of fighting. A woman is born to give birth to children, to nurture. Flying combat missions is against our nature; only the tragedy of our country made us join the army, to help our country, to help our people ... at the cornerstones

of our history, women were together with their men—they stood beside their men. To be in the army in crucial periods is one thing, but to want to be in the military is not quite natural for a woman.[39]

Despite the harsh conditions at the front and the masculine nature of their jobs, the airwomen did their best to maintain, their femininity. Fighter pilot Lidiya Litvyak reportedly decorated the inside of her cockpit with wildflowers and fashioned a colorful neck scarf from parachute material. Like the WASP, many of the Russian women pilots were stationed at mixed air bases, and relationships naturally developed between the young people. "We always tried to look good," said Popova. "We wore a little make-up even if it was forbidden. You only have your youth once. Ours came during the war, but still, we were not going to miss it."[40] A famous photograph taken by Yevgeny Khaldei of Popova and some of the women in her regiment shows the young Nadya primping for the camera before the attack at Novorossisk in September 1943. Pilot Yevgeniya Zhigulenko recounted a romantic view of herself as a young woman pilot preparing for a possible encounter with a potential suitor from a male airbase:

But life remains life and we, as military pilots, still remained young girls. We dreamed of our grooms, marriages, children, and a future happy, peaceful life. We thought to meet our future mates at the front. But our 46th Regiment was unique, for it was purely female. There wasn't even a shabby male mechanic to rest a glance on. Nevertheless, after a night of combat we never forgot to curl our hair. Some girls thought it unpatriotic to look unattractive. I argued that we should. I said, "Imagine that I have a forced landing at a male fighter airdrome. Soldiers are rushing to my aircraft because they know that the crew is female. I, absolutely dashing, slide out of the cockpit and take off my helmet, and my golden, curly hair streams down my shoulders. Everyone is awed by my dazzling beauty. They all desperately fall in love with me."[41]

Despite the frequency of male–female relationships at the front, sex was another matter entirely, according to many of the airwomen who were interviewed after the war. Author Shelley Saywell spoke to an unidentified woman veteran in her book *Women in War* who commented on the sex lives of young Russian soldiers:

There were certainly a lot of frontline love affairs, but obviously it was difficult to have sex. To do so you need the time and the place, and during the war we seldom had either. There was absolutely no privacy ...the conditions were hardly conducive to sex anyway. We were filthy, exhausted and hungry. We were just trying to survive. But there were a lot of cases when married men fell in love with girls at the front and never returned to their families afterwards. So we weren't entirely popular with everyone when the war ended.[42]

In contrast to the WASP, the Soviet airwomen received very little media attention during the war. The "Night Witches" of the 46th Guards Aviation Regiment got the most attention, probably because of the fact that they were the USSR's first all-female air regiment, and consequently, were viewed as the most vulnerable. The pilots of the 46th Regiment flew mostly the outdated wooden biplane, the Po-2, while the other regiments flew modern fighters and bombers. Men also flew the Po-2 into combat but were not referred to in print as "Eaglets" as the women flyers were. Instead, the male pilots were described in magazine articles as "Eagles" or "Falcons." Reina Pennington points out that the frequent use of the term "girl-pilots" (*devushki-letchiki*) further supports the idea that the women pilots were not regarded on equal terms with the men as Soviet propaganda preached. The Soviet male pilots were as young as the women, but the men were never described as "boy-pilots."[43] Even though the 46th Regiment received the most attention in the Soviet press, it was not a propaganda blitz. According to Rakobolskaya, the regiment's chief of staff, the first articles about the 46th Regiment actually changed their names to the masculine form. "It was like the regiment was a classified secret," she said. "Maybe they were afraid that we wouldn't be equal to the situation."[44] Or perhaps Stalin had a change of heart and became uncomfortable advertising the fact that Soviet women were fighting in combat at the front? Was the image of young Soviet girls dogfighting against Germany's best fighter aces high above the Motherland too much out of synch with Russian society's traditional views of women? There existed an obvious contradiction in the image of the "new" Soviet woman who was modern and independent, and the nurturing, domestic Russian woman who symbolized Mother Russia. The Soviet airwomen challenged both characterizations, and even after the war, proved difficult to classify by the socialist ideology professed by the USSR.

From the beginning, gender was at the very core of the Soviet women's regiments, as well as the WASP program. Despite being given the same combat assignments as male pilots during the war, the Soviet women flyers were viewed differently from their male counterparts. Partly because of the outdated planes they flew, the "Night Witches" of the Soviet Union's 46th Guards Night Bomber Aviation Regiment were seen as vulnerable. In the United States, the WASP received attention in the media that focused on their gender. In newspaper articles, the American public read about the seemingly glamorous lives of these "girl pilots." The airwomen recognized that their gender would be challenged in the military. Most of the pilots let the disapproving comments roll off their backs, and it made them even more determined to prove themselves in the air where their gender was not an issue. Throughout the duration of the war, the American and Soviet women pilots earned the respect of the aircrews they flew with. But winning over their countrymen proved more difficult as the war drew to a close.

The women aviators received unceremonious gratitude from their countries for filling a need created by the war, but history relegated them to footnotes. More than eighty years ago the American historian Henry Adams wrote in his autobiography, "The study of history is useful to the historian by teaching him his ignorance of woman; and the mass of this ignorance crushes one who is familiar enough with what are called historical sources to realize how few women have ever been known. The woman who is known only through a man is known wrong."[45] Until women in aviation are viewed without the curiosity that accompanies their involvement, their gender will continue to define their accomplishments. And this chapter in military history that has been predominantly known through men may finally be rewritten.

CHAPTER 5

The Ties That Bind

We were very young, and our friendship very warm, as it is now.
—Nadezhda Popova (Pilot, 46th Guards Night Bomber
Aviation Regiment)[1]

The severe strain that is placed on soldiers during a time of war draws them especially close to the individuals in their unit, and as a result, tight bonds of friendship often develop that last a lifetime. The WASP and the Soviet women pilots developed intimate and long-lasting relationships with the women with whom they served in World War II. Close ties formed between the women frequently as a result of the dangers that were inherent in their jobs as military pilots. More than sixty years after the war, the veterans (many of whom are now grandmothers and great-grandmothers) keep in regular contact with one another, reminiscing about their days in the war. Anne Noggle wrote about the special bond that exists between her fellow WASP:

> I thought about how few women have had the opportunity not only to fly for our Air Force, but to be thrown together willy-nilly in training and to know the bonding that usually is associated with groups who live and work in close proximity. This sense of belonging is all the more intense when the duties involve danger and risk. That makes it so rare with women. Add to that the kind of independent women we are and you have a portrait of a Women Airforce Service Pilot.[2]

Every two years the WASP hold a reunion in a different city in the United States. In an interview with the author, WASP Jean Downey Harman commented that the reunions are special times to reconnect with one's friends and former classmates. "There was such a close bonding among classmates," she said. "When I go to a reunion, the most important thing for me is to be with my classmates. We write each other often and e-mail," Harman said.[3] WASP Florence Shutsy-Reynolds added, "The camaraderie that we had extends even to today. It's like we're in the same brotherhood."[4]

Despite the noncombat status of their flying assignments in the war, the WASP were reminded all too often of the dangerous nature of their jobs. By June 1944, twenty-three WASP had crashed to their deaths. Most died because of mechanical failures of their aircraft and some as a result of mid-air collisions. During 1944, a WASP was killed almost every month.

In an interview with the author, Shutsy-Reynolds remembered the death of her classmate Beverly Moses. On July 18, 1944, less than a month after graduation, the plane Moses was copiloting crashed in the mountains near where she was stationed at Las Vegas Army Air Field in Nevada. "Her death was so unnecessary," Shutsy-Reynolds said. "We remember those who are no longer with us."[5]

Ann Baumgartner Carl recalled the news of the deaths of two trainees while at Avenger Field:

> One morning we awoke to our first deaths—two women pilots and an instructor lost on a night cross-country flight. The two women, Margaret Seip and Helen Severson, were best friends of Caryl Jones in my barracks. Caryl may have learned the details, but she did not talk about it, preferring to mourn in silence while she kept busy collecting together her friends' things to send to their families. The rest of us were saddened and sobered by their loss, by their absence. It forced us to look within and face our own mortality.[6]

Carl said that up until that time she and her fellow pilots had focused solely on flying well and practicing those things they did not do so well, like landings, steep turns, and holding altitude. They had never faced the actuality of death. "Now it suddenly hovered there in front of us," she said. "We could fail. We could die. Yet, we secretly felt 'it won't happen to me'... many of the women turned to their God—who for them was indeed their 'co-pilot.'"[7]

Two trainees were killed in 44-W-1, the WASP class of Anne Noggle. She adopted a stoic view of death during those years and said it was not something she and the other women pilots dwelled too much on. She wrote in an article for *Air & Space*: "I don't remember really talking about it among ourselves; we kept busy and we knew there would be losses. I think when you are doing something where there is risk, you don't let it into your conscious mind, at least I didn't. You made a pact with yourself that it might happen but probably not to you, and you are a fatalist—or you quit flying."[8]

Because of the WASP's civil servant and nonmilitary status in the USAAF, when one of their fellow flyers was killed, the government refused to pay for the remains to be shipped to their families for burial. Many WASP personally contributed money to have the bodies, as well as belongings, of their classmates sent home. A number of WASP even accompanied the coffins of their close friends on their final journey. Families of the deceased pilots were not given any insurance money, there was no flag placed on their coffin, and no gold star for their parents to hang in the window to show that their child had died in the war—all things provided for people who were officially a part of the military.

Dora Dougherty Strother said that although the deaths of her fellow WASP were upsetting, she tried to keep in mind that people were dying every day in the war. More than 50,000 men in the Army Air Forces ultimately perished in World War II.[9] One loss was particularly hard on Strother, and she recalled in the documentary film *Fly Girls,* the death of her friend Mabel Rawlinson at Camp Davis, which she witnessed up close:

> They were not able to get her out and so she burned inside her plane. The fire was intense. It was a very traumatic time for all of us here. There was an old nurse who came over to our barracks with a couple bottles of beer. She sat on the end of the barracks watching the fire, drinking her beer and singing old hymns...thinking the thoughts that we were all thinking.[10]

Strother, who later became a lieutenant colonel in the USAF (U.S. Air Force), acknowledged that death, however tragic, was part of the risk they all took being military pilots. "I think when you join the military you obviously go through a mindset that you're prepared for something like this... but this was the first time I had seen a friend die so it was a trauma for me and I think for all of us."[11] By the end of 1944 when the WASP were officially disbanded, thirty-eight women pilots had died in the service of their country.

The most dangerous flying assignments given to the WASP took place at Camp Davis in North Carolina. Here the women pilots flew missions to train antiaircraft artillery gunners. Camp Davis was a large base, and the fifty-two WASP who were assigned there were the only women working alongside thousands of men, many of whom strongly protested the arrival of the female flyers. WASP Eileen Roach discovered firsthand the dangers involved in target-towing missions. One day when Roach was halfway into her tow-target pattern at one end of the beach at about 1,500 feet, she began to see white specks zing past the nose of her plane and over the canopy. After several rounds she realized they were tracer bullets, non-live shells shot amidst the live ammunition to show gunners where they were aiming. Then she heard cracking sounds against the metal fuselage. She quickly got on the radio and said, "Hey, I think you are hitting me!" After several resounding metallic whacks, the bombardment stopped. A gunnery officer's voice crackled over the radio. "Sure am sorry," he said. "Some gunner down here thought he was supposed to shoot at the plane up there marked with that cloth marker. We got him straightened out." Roach flew a couple more passes of the beach and then turned back toward Camp Davis. When she climbed down out of the cockpit, she noticed four bullet holes in the fuselage within inches of where her head had been.[12]

After two WASP were killed at Camp Davis, Jacqueline Cochran flew there from Washington to investigate. The women pilots had repeatedly complained of having to fly planes that were in no condition to leave the ground. Several engines had quit in midair; eleven pilots had suffered forced landings. The tires on the planes, the WASP told Cochran, were so old that in one day there were five blowouts. Only a handful of the radios actually worked. The women also complained that their male instructors did not have enough flying experience to instruct them in the dangerous business of towing targets. When the leader of the WASP arrived at Camp Davis, she was met by a roomful of angry, frustrated, and anxious aviators, two of whom sent resignations to Cochran soon after her visit. Many of the WASP feared for their lives. They soon learned that in order to stay alive they would have to look out for themselves. Following the fatal crashes, the WASP routinely inspected their planes themselves.

After personally investigating Betty Taylor's death at Camp Davis, Cochran left quietly for Washington without discussing her findings with any of the WASP. What Cochran had found inside Taylor's demolished A-24 aircraft she could not make public. She feared jeopardizing her entire women's flying program if the truth became known. She would not reveal the details of the investigation even to the women pilots who were risking their lives at Camp Davis. In the gas tank of the airplane Cochran found traces of sugar. Sugar in sufficient quantities can stop an engine in seconds. She was convinced that the accident was caused by sabotage. Afraid of adverse publicity and a mutiny by the WASP on the base that would surely take place once the truth became known, Cochran never told her group of women flyers what caused the death of Taylor. From that day forward until the WASP were demobilized, controversy would surround them at Camp Davis.[13]

Among the thirty-eight WASP who were killed during the war, the body of Gertrude Tompkins Silver was never found. Thirty-two-year-old Silver took off from what is now Los Angeles International Airport on October 26, 1944, on a mission to deliver a P-51 Mustang to an air base in New Jersey. She and the aircraft she was flying were never seen or heard from again. Because her flight plan was misplaced, four days passed before anyone realized that she had not made it to the first leg of her cross-country trip. Recent searches for her crash site, which are ongoing, have involved divers, sonar

Jacqueline Cochran, director of the WASP program, during World War II. *Courtesy of the National Museum of the U.S. Air Force.*

Nancy Harkness Love, director of the Women's Auxiliary Ferrying Squadron (WAFS). *Courtesy of the National Museum of the U.S. Air Force.*

WASP trainees
Dorothy Bancroft,
Barbara Fleming,
and Sarabel Booth
at Avenger Field,
Sweetwater, Texas.
*Courtesy of The
Woman's Collection,
Texas Woman's
University.*

WASP trainees model their
oversized "zoot suits" at
Avenger Field. Caro
Bayley Bosca (43-W-7) is
pictured in the middle.
*Courtesy of The Woman's
Collection, Texas
Woman's University.*

Jacqueline Cochran with a group of WASP graduates from the class of 43-W-2 at the wishing well at Avenger Field. *Courtesy of The Woman's Collection, Texas Woman's University.*

WASP graduation day at Avenger Field, Sweetwater, Texas. *Courtesy of The Woman's Collection, Texas Woman's University.*

WASP on flight line at Laredo Army Air Field in Texas on January 22, 1944. *Courtesy of the National Archives.*

WASP Elsie Dyer with a male pilot on the wing of an A-25 Helldiver at Camp Davis, North Carolina. *Courtesy of the National Museum of the U.S. Air Force.*

Scott Army Air Base in Gary, Indiana. Left to right: WASP May Ball (43-W-8), Jana Crawford (43-W-8), and Mary Estill (43-W-8). A P-51 Mustang is in the background. *Courtesy of The Woman's Collection, Texas Woman's University.*

Lockbourne Army Air Base in Columbus, Ohio. Left to right: WASP Frances Green (43-W-5), Margaret Kirchner (43-W-6), Ann Waldner (43-W-6), and Blanche Osborne (43-W-6) with the B-17 "Pistol Packin' Mama" named in honor of the women pilots. *Courtesy of The Woman's Collection, Texas Woman's University.*

WASP Shirley Slade at the controls of a B-26 at Harlingen Army Air Field in Texas. *Courtesy of the National Museum of the U.S. Air Force.*

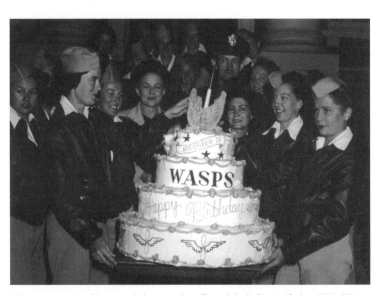

The women pilots celebrate the first birthday of the WASP on November 16, 1943, in Courthouse Square, Sweetwater, Texas. *Courtesy of the National Museum of the U.S. Air Force.*

Maxwell Field in Montgomery, Alabama. Left to right: WASP Elizabeth MacKethan Magid (44-W-2), Mildred Davidson Dalrymple (44-W-4), Eloise Huffhines Bailey (44-W-4), and Clara Jo Marsh (44-W-3). *Courtesy of The Woman's Collection, Texas Woman's University.*

Jane Straughan, a graduate of the first WASP class of 43-W-1, walks towards an AT-6 at Houston Municipal Airport in Houston, Texas. *Courtesy of the National Archives.*

Four WASP review a map on the wing of an AT-6. *Courtesy of The Woman's Collection, Texas Woman's University.*

Jacqueline Cochran leans against the prop of a P-51 Mustang after the war. *Courtesy of the National Museum of the U.S. Air Force.*

The WASP traveled to Moscow in 1990 to meet the Soviet women veterans. Pictured here are, left to right: WASP Charlyne Creger, Barbara Ward Lazarsky, Marjorie Osborne Nicol, and Marty Wyall, with Nadezhda Popova, a pilot in the 46th Guards Night Bomber Aviation Regiment. *Courtesy of The Woman's Collection, Texas Woman's University.*

Pilot Nataliya Meklin of the 46th Guards Night Bomber Aviation Regiment, and a Hero of the Soviet Union. *Courtesy of Timeline Films.*

Marina Raskova in her leather flight helmet and goggles before the war. *Courtesy of Timeline Films.*

Marina Raskova is honored in Moscow for her record-setting flight in 1938. *Courtesy of Timeline Films.*

September 1943. Night bomber pilots Irina Sebrova (seated in center) and Nadezhda Popova (standing), with navigator Vera Belik (seated at far right) in Novorossiysk. *Courtesy of Timeline Films.*

Po-2 with rear-facing machine gun, dropping leaflets. The plane has been painted with the phrase: "To avenge our comrades, Tanya Makarova and Vera Belik!" *Courtesy of Timeline Films.*

Pilot Evdokiya Nikulina (left) and navigator Yevgeniya Rudneva of the 46th Guards Night Bomber Aviation Regiment in front of their Po-2 aircraft. *Courtesy of Timeline Films.*

Left to right: Pilot Marina Chechneva, navigator Lidiya Svistunova of the 46th Guards Night Bomber Aviation Regiment, and an unidentified airwoman, prior to flight, wearing heavy, oversized flight suits. *Courtesy of Timeline Films.*

A member of the 46th Guards Night Bomber Aviation Regiment is decorated during a military ceremony. *Courtesy of Timeline Films.*

Ground and aircrews of the 125th Guards Dive Bomber Aviation Regiment in front of a Pe-2 aircraft. Standing, sixth from left: pilot Antonina Spitsina Bondareva; seventh from left: navigator Yevgeniya Guruleva-Smironova, and standing at far right: navigator Galina Brok-Beltsova. *Courtesy of Timeline Films.*

Lidiya Litvyak, the Soviet Union's most famous woman fighter ace. *Courtesy of Timeline Films.*

Left to right: Fighter pilots Lidiya Litvyak, Ekaterina Budanova, and Mariya Kuznetsova. *Courtesy of Timeline Films.*

Pilots of the 586th Fighter Aviation Regiment. *Courtesy of Timeline Films.*

A Soviet woman aviator enjoys a quiet moment in front of her Yak fighter aircraft. *Courtesy of Timeline Films.*

A group of Soviet airwomen look through a fashion magazine during a break from the fighting in World War II. *Courtesy of Timeline Films.*

A group of Soviet veterans stand in front of a statue of Marina Raskova in the city of Engels where the women's aviation regiments trained during the war. *Courtesy of Timeline Films.*

technology, and a sub-bottom profiler in the area off Santa Monica Bay where she is believed to have gone down. In the meantime, the six-decades-old mystery of what happened to WASP Silver remains unsolved.

The Soviet women pilots who flew combat missions throughout the war faced life and death situations on a daily basis. Death was a very real possibility, and the young women in their own way had to reconcile with it and learn to live with the fear. As a result of their perilous flying assignments, extremely close bonds of friendship formed between the women. The Soviets did not publish precise figures on women's wartime casualties, but according to the regimental histories compiled by the women pilots themselves after the war, it is believed that more than fifty women in Marina Raskova's three air regiments were killed in action. Regardless of how frequently it occurred, the death of a comrade-in-arms was something the airwomen never grew accustomed to. Popova remembered the constant fear she and her fellow pilots experienced during the war:

> We were frightened all the time. You didn't think about it during the flight, but later. We flew each night, and all through those years never slept enough. There was an enormous strain on the nerves. I would see images of burning planes crashing with my girlfriends in them whenever I closed my eyes. I hoped that if my time came it would be an instantaneous death. The thought of being severely disfigured scared me much more. I was young and pretty, and I wanted all the things every young girl wants. I wanted to live a life I would not be ashamed of if I survived.[14]

The night bombing pilots of the 46th Regiment flew without parachutes so that the lightweight planes could carry an extra load—about 550–660 pounds of bombs per sortie. It was a precarious trade off, but one the pilots did not question. Another reason for not having parachutes may have been that the pilots flew their bombers so low to the ground to make the use of parachutes impossible. The hazards of flying at the front drew the women aviators together, and the veterans today emphasize the strong emotional bonds they experienced with their colleagues. Women in the 46th Regiment appear to have been especially close to one another. "Our regiment was very harmonious and close-knit," wrote Polina Gelman. "We were like sisters. So we have passed through our entire lives. Right to the present we rely on one another as if we were family."[15] Historian Christine White drew comparisons between the Soviet women pilots and the WASP in her introduction to Anne Noggle's book *A Dance with Death: Soviet Airwomen in World War II*. She commented about the unique relationships that developed between the women flyers: "There is also a striking degree of similarity between the two groups in the camaraderie that the women shared. There is a closeness—a community of being—that approaches the relationship of family. It is not surprising to note that both groups developed their strongest ties during periods of great stress: the WASP during their training, and the Soviet women while in the field."[16]

The worst night of combat for the 46th Regiment came on July 31, 1943, when four crews (eight women) were lost to German fighters. In remembering the event, Serafima Amosova-Taranenko, a pilot and deputy commander of the 46th Regiment, remarked: "You can imagine our feelings when we returned to our quarters and saw eight beds folded, and we knew they were the beds of our friends who perished a few hours ago. It was impossible not to cry. It was a great loss and pain but none of us surrendered, and we were full of anger and decided to pay the enemy back for the loss of our friends."[17]

For the women who witnessed the final moments of their friends' lives that summer night, the horrific images remained vivid in their minds for many decades after the war. Mariya Smirnova recalled watching the planes "burn like sheets of paper." "We were not equipped with parachutes at that time, so eight girls burned in the air," she said. "It is a horrible scene when a plane is burning. First it explodes; then it burns like a torch falling apart, and you can see particles of fuselage, wings, tail, and human bodies scattered in the air."[18]

In an interview after the war, Irina Rakobolskaya, chief of staff for the 46th Regiment, recalled the stresses the women aircrews faced flying nighttime sorties. "Flying ten missions, you'd be in the air ten hours at a stretch, with small intervals for landing and take-off. Sometimes a girl's plane would be set on fire and would fall like a flaming torch before her friends' eyes. It took only a match to set our planes alight."[19]

Serafima Amosova-Taranenko was proud of the courage and skill exhibited by the women in her unit. Every pilot, she said, understood the dangers they faced in combat, but it was a danger they generally kept to themselves. She recounted to Noggle in her book on the Soviet women aviators:

> To fly a combat mission is not a trip under the moon. Every attack, every bombing is a dance with death. In spite of this, every girl knew the danger, and none refused to fly her mission or used a pretext to avoid participating in the bombing. Our feelings were that we were doing a simple job, just a job to save our country, to liberate it from the enemy. I don't know what was in the hearts of these girls when they were climbing into and sitting in the cockpit before their flight. I don't know, but you could not read on their faces any fear or feeling of danger, and they performed their duty with an open heart and very honestly and bravely.[20]

Over a period of time, the pilots created rituals in an attempt to deal psychologically with their stress when fellow airwomen were known missing or presumed dead. Olga Yerokhina-Averjanova, a mechanic in the 46th Regiment, remembered: "On the night of a crash, we never slept, never left the airfield. We waited until dawn, believing in miracles, asking God to save our girls, waiting for them to return. Many of them did not come back, but sometimes when the planes were missing after a mission they really did return. They were shot down and made emergency landings, returning sometimes two or three days later."[21]

When some members of the regiment failed to return from a nightly mission, their plates and silverware were put out for them in the mess the next morning even when it was known that they had been shot down. Their places, according to pilot Raisa Zhitova-Yushina, were set for several days in the hope that they would return. Oftentimes superstitions replaced the religious faith that was forbidden in Soviet Russia. But just as the state's propaganda that upheld the image of the "new" Soviet woman often conflicted with reality, so did the idea that religious belief did not exist among the airwomen. Judging by the interviews of the veterans, there were women in the regiments who prayed to God to keep them and their fellow flyers safe. For those who denounced religion, photographs of family members were often a replacement, brought along in the cockpit for strength and comfort.

When a pilot was killed, her body was buried under the airfield and a brief ceremony was held to honor her memory. The women planted flowers in the mounds of dirt that covered their comrade's body in a loving tribute. Rows of mounds along the airfield became a familiar sight. Yevgeniya "Zhenya" Rudneva, a navigator in the 46th Regiment, recorded in her diary on March 29, 1944, the burial of two pilots from her unit. "Yesterday we had weather appropriate for a funeral: it rained all day and in the evening. The girls were buried to the accompaniment of an orchestra and the salute of twenty rifles."[22] Rudneva was killed a week later on April 8, 1944, on her 645th combat mission.[23]

Every year since the end of World War II, the survivors of Marina Raskova's three air regiments meet on the second day of May in a small park in front of Moscow's Bolshoi Theater to remember old times and honor their fallen comrades. Probably the most memorable reunion for the Soviet women pilots took place in May 1990 when a group of over forty WASP traveled to the USSR to meet the Russian combat pilots about whom they had only heard rumors about during the war. The historic meeting between the world's first female military pilots was featured in a November 1990 article in *Soviet Woman*. Barbara Lazarsky, then president of the WASP, was quoted as saying, "We are grateful to you for having been our allies. We hope to remain friends."[24] WASP Marion Stegeman Hodgson recalled meeting the Soviet airwomen in her book: "The best reunion of all was when a group of us went to the USSR in May 1990 to meet Soviet women pilots, our sisters in World War II who flew combat. For us, the Cold War ended that May."[25]

WASP Noggle traveled to the Soviet Union in the fall of 1990 to interview and photograph sixty-nine of the Russian women veterans. At a special banquet held in her honor, Noggle, who represented her fellow WASP, was made an honorary member of the 125th Guards Bomber Aviation Regiment. According to Noggle, the WASP had often imagined how they would have fared if they had been called upon to fly in combat during the war. Noggle recorded her thoughts of her trip to meet the Russian women in the preface of her book *A Dance with Death:*

> I thought then, on my way to their country, that these stories would cut across all boundaries and that our gender-relatedness was a key —our sameness as girls and women, past and present would be more significant than our differing cultural backgrounds. That proved to be true. As they told their stories, their voices and gestures spoke even before the translated words. For people held mute for almost all the years of their lives by terror and despotism, the communication of the spirit has never been silenced.[26]

During her trip to the USSR to meet the Soviet women veterans, Noggle discovered that she and her fellow WASP shared much in common with their Russian counterparts. Despite the dissimilarities in wartime flying missions, military status, and political ideologies, the female flyers were connected not only by gender but also by a fervent desire to serve their country in its hour of need. The close friendships that developed between these pilots while performing perilous airborne missions during World War II continue to this day.

CHAPTER 6

The WASP Are Disbanded

You don't need legislation to prove something...you can be whatever
you set your heart and head to be, and don't let anybody tell you you
can't be, because 1,078 women pilots did it in World War II.
                    —WASP Annelle Henderson Bulechek (44-W-2)[1]

In 1944 as an allied victory became more certain, articles in the American
media began to reflect a concern for the postwar economy and encouraged
a return to prewar values, which placed women in the home rather than in
the factories and in the military. Articles on women in the military became
sharply critical as the war reached its end. No longer revered as patriotic
symbols, these women were viewed as threats to men returning from overseas and a detriment to the postwar economy. Unfortunately for the WASP,
it was in this climate that they attempted to gain militarization.

   From the very beginning, the WASP were told that the program would be
militarized, and they performed and were evaluated as if they already were
members of the armed forces. "We fully expected that we were going to be
in the military when we joined," remembered WASP Marty Wyall.[2] WASP
were subject to military customs and procedures. They wore uniforms,
marched, and saluted. The differences were that the female pilots did not
receive the same benefits of those who were in the military, and they could
quit their positions at any time. As civilians, WASP were not entitled to
the hospitalization, death, or veterans' benefits as the male pilots they served
with, nor did they receive the same pay, housing, or living expenditures. In
April 1944, eighty-five WASP were sent to officer training school in
Orlando, Florida, in anticipation of their becoming Army officers.[3] That

same spring the WASP were issued new Santiago blue uniforms. To the women pilots, militarization seemed just around the corner.

As far back as 1942, numerous avenues were being explored to militarize the WASP. One suggestion was to place the WASP under the control of the WAC. Jacqueline Cochran, however, strongly disliked WAC director Oveta Culp Hobby, and she rejected the idea outright. Cochran reportedly said about Hobby: "I will not serve under a woman who doesn't know her ass from a propeller."[4]

It was concluded in August 1943 that the only way for the WASP to be "brought into the U.S. Army Air Forces so as to have them comply with the requirements...is to have separate legislation passed providing for the establishment of a new military division of the Army Air Forces."[5] As a result, the USAAF began work on a bill to establish the women pilots as a militarized unit of the Air Forces. Despite warnings that Congress was becoming increasingly hostile to legislation of this nature, the USAAF believed the bill was the WASP's last remaining option.

In 1944, when the USAAF brought the WASP bill before Congress, two major obstacles existed: a Congress that was concerned more with cutting military expenses than with creating new programs, and the thousands of men who wanted the flying positions then held by the WASP. The latter would ultimately draw public attention to the actions of Congress. The male civilian pilots, who had then recently been laid off and were then subject to draft into the walking Army, organized a powerful lobby against the WASP bill. The opposition led by the male pilots, teamed with the increasingly negative publicity in the media about the WASP, ultimately led to the disbandment of the women's flying program.

As a result of the pressure applied by the male civilian pilots, the House Civil Service Investigating Committee began an inquiry into the WASP training program. The investigation was highly publicized in the media. An article in the *Washington Times Herald* distorted the facts about the WASP, making their achievements irrelevant, and instead emphasized the women's gender: "Miss Cochran, who in peacetime was never too busy gathering up both men's and women's flying trophies to neglect her own femininity, is also determined that the women flying for the ATC shall not neglect their feminine allure. She has ordered them out of slacks and dungarees and into dresses at least four nights a week at the Sweetwater, Texas, Training Post."[6]

Newspaper accounts of the women pilots that had once been positive grew critical as opposition to the WASP bill attracted the attention of the American public. An article by the Chicago Tribune Press Service titled "Army Passes Up Jobless Pilots to Train Wasps: Prefers Women to Older, Experienced Flyers" began: "With 5,000 experienced airplane pilots looking for jobs as a result of the liquidation of the civil aeronautic commission's pilot training program, the government is training more than 1,000 young women, at an estimated cost of $6 million, as ferry pilots for the army."[7] Supporters of the displaced CAA male pilots were quick to emphasize the cost of the WASP program and seldom mentioned the actual wartime service carried out by the women flyers.

Articles about the proposed legislation to militarize the WASP frequently focused more on the plight of male civilian pilots than on the WASP. Realizing that opposition to militarizing the WASP was largely based on the concern for the male pilots, Secretary of War Henry Stimson began to address the issue. He stated that the purpose of the legislation was not to give women special privileges, nor to prevent skilled male pilots from flying, but to allow the military to take full advantage of the wartime contribution of women pilots.[8]

Cochran, determined to control her WASP program that was then fighting for its very existence, forbade the women pilots from speaking with the media or publicly discussing the bill before Congress. "In the last twelve to fourteen months of our service in World War II, an edict came down from headquarters that there was to be no publicity and no media interviews or anything about the WASP or by the WASP," said WASP Madge Rutherford Minton.[9] One can only imagine the frustration the women pilots experienced reading the negative reports about them in the press and being unable to respond to them. The slander aimed at the WASP resulted in many letters to Cochran from her airwomen who were shocked by the negative publicity campaign that was being waged against them. WASP Isabel Fenton wrote to Cochran in August 1944:

> Your distress, we know, must be greater than ours, but I am writing to find out what we can do about our existing situation. There has been no favorable publicity about us at all with the possible exception of *Time* magazine's backhanded reference to the "hard working, rule abiding but expensive WASPs." We know the things printed are not true and we would like to have them
>
> Refuted...why don't we get somebody who'll come out with the truth about us?[10]

The WASP were accused of being excessively glamorous. When their new uniforms were issued in late spring 1944, it resulted in unfavorable media attention. A *Washington, D.C. Star* article emphasized the alleged exclusiveness of the women's uniforms:

> An exclusive Fifth Avenue shop is outfitting the War Department's women flyers in snappy new military uniforms at $505 per WASP, a Senate Military Affairs Subcommittee was told yesterday. By contrast, Mr. Morrison said, the flying instructors being thrown out of jobs by

cutbacks in USAAF pilot training look a bit ragged in old khaki pants and "Woodtick" coats discarded by the CCC.[11]

According to information compiled by WASP Byrd Howell Granger in her book *On Final Approach: The Women Airforce Service Pilots of WWII*, each of the WASP's Santiago blue uniforms cost the United States Government $326.06. Additionally, the women pilots were expected to pay for the required flannel shirts, neckties, shoes, socks, stockings, handbag, underclothing, gloves, and a black and white dress, themselves, estimated at costing at least $100.[12] The WASP were proud of their uniforms, as they helped to give the women pilots the legitimacy among military personnel that they craved.

The year before, on September 30, 1943, Representative John Costello of California introduced the first WASP militarization bill, House Resolution 3358. It would be six months before the Committee on Military Affairs held hearings on the bill. In the meantime, Costello submitted a longer bill, House Resolution 4219. This bill was constructed similarly to the first bill, except that it provided greater detail concerning the administration of the WASP program.

On March 22, 1944, the hearing by the Committee on Military Affairs took place and lasted less than one hour with only USAAF Commanding General H.H. "Hap" Arnold testifying. Arnold reiterated that the passage of the bill was important not only so that the USAAF could expand the WASP program and eventually replace all male pilots domestically but also to enable the USAAF to utilize more effectively WASP who were already active.[13] That same day the committee issued a report recommending the passage of House Resolution 4219. According to the report, the committee recognized the personnel shortages that warranted the expansion of the WASP program as well as the insurance and medical benefits the women pilots deserved as members of the armed forces. Two days later, Senators Joseph Hill of Alabama and Harold Burton of Ohio submitted Senate Resolution 1810, "A bill to provide for the appointment of female pilots and aviation cadets in the Air Forces of the Army." Senate Resolution 1810 was the Senate version of House Resolution 4219 and contained the same elements as the House bill.[14] Expectations for the passage of the bill looked promising, especially because Congress had never rejected a piece of legislation supported by the War Department or commanding generals during the war.

Between March and June 1944, however, the male civilian pilots began to receive considerable sympathetic coverage in the media. The male military pilots returning from combat overseas also wanted to guarantee their flight pay, and so they joined the civilian pilots in their attack against the WASP. As several civil aviation organizations and veterans' associations joined their cause, they formed a formidable lobby against the women pilots. The male pilots convinced Representative Robert Ramspeck, who chaired the

Committee on the Civil Service, to investigate the WASP. The thirteen-page report that became known as the Ramspeck Report was created without any members of the investigating committee visiting the WASP's training school at Avenger Field or any bases to which WASP were assigned to active duty.[15]

Unfortunately for the airwomen, the misleading and often erroneous findings in the Ramspeck Report made their way into the nation's newspapers and magazines, and had considerable influence on the members of Congress, who would ultimately determine the fate of the female flyers. Representative James Morrison of Louisiana voiced particularly strong opposition to the WASP bill and entered the entire Ramspeck Report into the public record. Morrison used newspaper opinion pieces and editorials to bolster opposition to the bill. One article quoted by a congressman went so far as to allege that the USAAF was backing the WASP program only because Cochran had seduced General Arnold. "In the last week the shapely pilot has seen her coveted commission coming closer and closer...one of the highest placed generals, it seems gazed into her eyes, and since then has taken her cause celebre very much 'to heart'...she's such an attractive composition of wind-blown bob, smiling eyes and outdoor skin nobody blames him."[16]

From a carefully guarded top secret experiment, the WASP had overnight become notorious in the country at large. Even some American servicemen seemed to enjoy the opportunity to harass a particular woman pilot. Having delivered a P-47 to North Carolina, WASP Jill McCormick was sitting in the lobby of a hotel in Raleigh reading while she waited for the departure of her commercial flight back to her home base in New Castle, Delaware. She was suddenly surrounded by a group of men in uniform who shouted at her, "Go back home WASP, we don't need you! You're in a crummy organization, it shouldn't even exist." Then they called her a slut.[17] The WASP were bewildered by the negative attention they were suddenly receiving. Despite the unsolicited attacks, the women knew that they had important duties to perform and continued to focus on their flying assignments.

On June 20, 1944, House Resolution 4219, the Costello Bill, was introduced for consideration, and the following day debates took place on the House floor that centered primarily on the dilemma of the male civilian pilots and not on the WASP. The original purpose for the bill, to militarize the WASP, seemed to be lost then in Congress's desire to placate the demands of the CAA pilots. Supporters of the WASP then sensed that their battle was lost. A vote on June 21, 1944, quickly confirmed their fears, and the legislation that would have militarized the women pilots and made them legitimate members of the armed forces was effectively killed in Congress by a margin of only nineteen votes. Social pressure, as well as cultural fears released by the anticipated end of the war, attributed to the defeat of the WASP bill. It did not help matters either that many of the

congressmen were veterans themselves who identified with the plight of the
displaced male pilots.

On June 26, 1944, upon his return from Europe after directing the air
attacks for the D-day invasion, General Arnold ordered that the WASP
training program be discontinued as soon as those currently in classes finished. The next class of WASP, who were scheduled to start training just
four days after Arnold issued his order, were sent a telegram informing them
that because of the recommendations of the House Civil Service Committee
and the unfavorable action of the House of Representatives on the WASP
bill, their orders to report for WASP training were cancelled.[18] Unfortunately, the telegrams came too late for many of the trainees who had already
arrived in Sweetwater, Texas. Betty Stagg Turner, who graduated in the second to last WASP class, remembered the women pilots who were forced to
return home: "When the girls that would have been in 45-1 came in, and
were told, it was terrible. Some of them had sold their homes, because they
were going into the service; some of them had made arrangements for their
children; and there were so many things that just broke our hearts. It was
so sad for us."[19]

Until the WASP were officially disbanded on December 20, 1944, they
continued to receive harsh treatment in the press. In an October 1944 issue
of *Contact*, a leading aviation magazine, nineteen-year-old Mary Elizabeth
McConnell, who had the misfortune of having been accepted into the WASP
program just as it was announced that it would be disbanded, wrote a letter
to the editor in support of the WASP. McConnell lamented the discrimination women faced in the area of aviation: "I know someday women will
come into their own in the field of flying. However, it grieves me to think
that even today with so much belief in 'women's equality,' so much
opposition exists in the field of flying against them."[20] Interestingly, the
response to her letter by the magazine's editor, clearly illustrates the type
of intolerance for the WASP that continued late in the war. The editor
wrote:

> Opposing the WASP Training Program was a service to aviation and
> to our country. It just didn't make sense to have several thousand male
> pilots cleaning beer vats, tending bar, driving taxi cabs—yes, even sev-
> eral hundred of them on unemployment relief—all able, experienced
> pilots and at the same time be throwing away several million dollars
> to train young girls as pilots. Only a few ever qualified to handle big
> planes.[21]

The magazine's editor went on to write: "Something else you may not
know—twenty-three of these girls were killed. Something else you may not
know—scores of them were on any number of occasions grounded for several days because they could not take off a grasshopper plane in a stiff

wind." In his condescending tone, he continued to discredit the WASP, emphasizing their gender:

> We do feel however, that glamour had something to do with the desire of many of them to displace these experienced men pilots. To those who are anxious to render service to their country…Uncle Sam is still desperately in need of nurses and cadet nurses to care for our boys who are falling in action all over the world. That is where the feminine touch is really needed—of course, there is no glamour—only downright rub and scrub work when you put on a nurse's uniform.[22]

According to author Molly Merryman, the story of the disbandment of the WASP is one in which ignorance and fear dominated decision making, and in which cultural assumptions about gender had more influence than the facts surrounding the women's actual involvement in wartime efforts.[23] The issue, she points out, was clearly not about the WASP as pilots, but about women who were going beyond culturally constructed boundaries of how women were expected to behave, and who were serving in what were perceived to be male roles. Despite the support of the War Department and the Army Air Forces, American society, as represented by Congress and the media, had determined that the war was all but over and that emphasis should now be placed on returning the country to a peacetime structure. In this ideological construction, there was no place for the WASP because their continued existence would have symbolized a war that was not yet won, a shift in the roles allowed to women, or both.[24]

Additionally, one cannot ignore the irony that the CAA, the same organization that first gave so many women the opportunity to earn their wings before the war, would be the same organization that aggressively lobbied against the WASP in 1944 and helped to take their wings away. Women flyers were not a threat, it was believed, so long as they filled a temporary void left by male pilots. Public favor turned against the WASP when it was alleged that they would ultimately replace the men.

The WASP were stunned and disillusioned when news reached them that they soon would be released from duty. "So we just had to go home," remembered Barbara Erickson London. The morning she left her base in Long Beach, California, "There were fifty-one aircraft sitting on the runway that didn't get delivered that day." WASP Faith Buchner Richards added, "The war was still going on…that was the thing that hurt. We couldn't contribute."[25]

London, who was awarded the Air Medal by General Arnold in 1943 for making four 2,000-mile trips in only five days to deliver four aircraft, recalled later how essential ferry pilots were to the war effort. "The pursuits were so badly needed that the ferry pilots had what they called a 'number two priority' on the airlines," she said. "The only person who could kick

us off a seat on an airplane was the President of the United States. If we had
to get home after delivering an airplane we could bump anybody, including
senators, congressmen and cabinet members because we were ferry pilots.
We were that badly needed."[26]

Jean Downey Harman flew only two months on active duty before the
WASP were sent home. "We were all brokenhearted," she recalled. "I don't
know why we were really disbanded, but it was very disappointing. And
worse than anything was just to leave us without anything, no GI Bill, no
nothing."[27] It is interesting to note that the day after the WASP bill was
defeated in Congress, on June 22, 1944, President Roosevelt signed into
law the GI Bill of Rights. If the WASP had achieved militarization, they
too would have been eligible to enjoy the benefits of this new law: life insurance, educational assistance, home mortgages, and medical coverage.

It was particularly demoralizing to the women pilots that they were deactivated at a time when their services were still needed in the war. On the day
the women pilots were disbanded, hundreds of aircraft throughout the
country sat on runways undelivered. WASP Jean Moore recalled:

> When we were going to be sent home the pilots who had flown their
> missions and returned didn't want to do what we'd been doing. They
> wanted to fly their four hours a month and get their flight pay. They
> didn't want to take a BT up and test it. The day we were to leave, the
> twentieth of December, some depot called and said, "We've got five
> airplanes to be tested." We said, "Sorry, you'll have to get your little
> boys to do them." We were necessary...we were useful.[28]

General Arnold and Cochran addressed more than 100 WASP on active
duty who had returned to Sweetwater, Texas on December 7, 1944, exactly
three years after the attack on Pearl Harbor, to attend the last WASP graduation. "The emotions of happiness and sorrow are pretty close together, and
today I am experiencing them both at the same time, as well as the third
emotion of pride," Cochran told the women pilots.[29] "What the WASP have
done is without precedent in the history of the world."[30] Arnold, who had
led a valiant battle for the WASP's militarization, had nothing but praise
for the female flyers. "We of the Army Air Forces are proud of you; we will
never forget our debt to you," Arnold told the pilots gathered at Avenger
Field, many of whom never flew a single mission as a WASP. The commanding general went on to describe the merits of the WASP program:

> I want to stress how valuable I believe this whole WASP program has
> been. If another national emergency arises—let us hope it does not,
> but let us this time face the possibility—if it does, we will not again
> look upon a women's flying organization as an experiment. We will
> know that they can handle our fastest fighters, our heaviest bombers;

we will know that they are capable of ferrying, target towing, flying training, test flying, and the countless other activities which you have proved you can do.[31]

After the emotionally charged graduation ceremony, the WASP of 44-10 found themselves wandering around the airfield with nothing to do but pack their bags and prepare to return home. The following day, Colonel Roy P. Ward, Avenger Field's last commanding officer, ordered his women pilots in flying gear and assembled them on the flight line. "We're closing down the field, as you well know," he told the WASP. "Those PTs and BTs out there have to go down to San Angelo to be stored. I have no written orders to ferry them, but you're trained ferry pilots, and you're going to have at least one flight to your credit." [32] It was a risky move that could have jeopardized his military career, but Colonel Ward saw in the delighted faces of the women pilots before him that he had made the right decision. Ward followed his WASP in the official Avenger Field plane, a twin-engine transport called the *Fifinella,* with the Disney-designed female gremlin painted on its nose. An hour later all WASP landed without incident at their destination, and Ward signed over the trainers to the operations office. The women pilots hitched a ride back to Sweetwater in the transport, and when the plane reached Avenger Field, they did something they had always wanted to do—they buzzed the tower. This last defiant action by the WASP came to symbolize the final flight of *Fifinella.*

There was nothing left for the WASP to do then but return home. Florence Shutsy-Reynolds, who had been stationed at Merced Army Air Field, recalled her long journey home to Pennsylvania from her base in California following the disbanding of the WASP. "I made it back home on ten dollars and twenty-five cents," she said.[33] Shutsy-Reynolds traveled with another WASP who was going home to Philadelphia. The two women rode on military aircraft as far as they could go, and the rest of the way they went by bus. The Red Cross sold them coffee and donuts on their eastward journey. Shutsy-Reynolds finally arrived home on Christmas Day after a long bus ride sitting atop her parachute.

Many of the WASP hoped to continue flying in some capacity after the war, but for the majority of them, their wings had been forever clipped. Cochran herself was at a loss as to what the women pilots would be able to do after they no longer were flying for the military. "The future of women in aviation will not be on the airlines," she admitted in a *New York Times* article on November 5, 1944, "but perhaps on feeder lines, in aerial photography, crop dusting and instructing."[34] Cochran also saw her pilots being utilized to help sell aviation to the women of America who still made up a small percentage of airlines travelers. Although still involved in her cosmetics business, Cochran was hired as a director of North East Airlines in December, to help attract more female passengers, a position similar to what was filled by Amelia Earhart fifteen years earlier at Transcontinental Air Transport. It appeared that one of the world's most daring and accomplished female aviators was again being relegated to the airlines' marketing department.

The airlines did offer jobs to the former WASP, but they were usually recruited as stewardesses. "I was as qualified as some of the guys," recalled WASP Barbara Erickson London. "But the airlines just sent me back an application for being a stewardess."[35] WASP Jean Downey Harman applied to American Airlines after the war, but was told she too would be considered only for a stewardess position. "Airlines companies were hesitant to hire young women in those days because they thought they might get engaged and then would quit their job," Harman said.[36]

WASP Vivian Cadman Eddy, who graduated in the 43-W-5 class, worked as a stewardess for two years after the WASP disbanded. "I remember the girl saying, 'How can you possibly want to be a stewardess when you can fly the airplane?'" Eddy recalled. "Well, I said, 'You won't hire me as a pilot.'"[37]

Remarkably, ten years earlier, Helen Richey, who flew with the ATA and WASP during the war, became the first woman to be given the opportunity to pilot a scheduled airliner when she was hired by Central Airlines. Richey was also the first woman to be sworn in as a United States air mail pilot that same year. Richey did not have long, however, to enjoy her flying position at the airlines. She was soon forced to resign her post at Central Airlines by the all-male pilots union. Not until the 1970s would small numbers of women begin to pilot planes for commercial airlines and the USAF.

The WASP who returned home continued their studies at university, began careers outside of aviation, married, had children, and some continued to fly recreationally throughout their lives. In 1947, when the USAF was created as a separate branch of the armed forces, several WASP joined the Air Force Reserves as officers. Although they were not allowed to fly, the women wanted to continue serving their country in the military. According to WASP Anne Noggle, in 1949 the Air Force offered commissions to all former WASP, and 150 women accepted the commissions, while twenty-five of them went on to become career officers.[38] Women had to wait another thirty years before they were allowed in the cockpits of military aircraft.

"Our legacy is that we opened the door," said WASP Shutsy-Reynolds. "Jacqueline Cochran called the WASP jobs 'dishwasher' jobs, but someone had to do them—why not women?"[39] Betty Jane Williams from the WASP class 44-W-6 retired from the USAF as a lieutenant colonel. "We didn't think about the fact that we were playing role models, but now that we look back on it we're all glad we did."[40]

WASP Ruth Woods, who continued flying after the war, recognized the important precedent she and her fellow female flyers set for women aviators today: "We opened the door for the present women in the Air Force and other women in aviation," she said. "We opened that door so that they would be accepted and not sneered at. We laid the groundwork. We followed behind people like Amelia Earhart, who were loners. We came in as a body, a group—any group can exert more pressure than a single individual. I personally feel that was our greatest accomplishment."[41]

CHAPTER 7

Demobilization of the Soviet Airwomen

Our friendship has been preserved until the present day. Youth is youth. We made pillows out of our foot cloths and embroidered the Pe-2 on them. When it came time for our last farewell at the end of the war, we could not imagine how we could go on living without each other. We made a good family.

—Ekaterina Petrovna Chuikova (Mechanic, 125th Guards Bomber Aviation Regiment)[1]

On May 9, 1945, Germany surrendered, signaling the end of the war in Europe. At ten past one in the morning the voice of Radio Moscow's chief announcer, Yuri Levitan, announced: "Attention, this is Moscow. Germany has capitulated...this day, in honor of the victorious Great Patriotic War, is to be a national holiday, a festival of victory." Stalin spoke briefly to the jubilant crowds that evening: "My dear fellow countrymen and women. I am proud today to call you my comrades. Your courage has defeated the Nazis. The war is over...now we shall build a Russia fit for heroes and heroines."[2]

Not long after the war ended, a decree was issued demobilizing all Soviet women from military service except for a few specialists.[3] For the most part, women were rapidly discharged from the Soviet military after the war, and were subsequently banned from service academies, which was virtually the only way to become a military pilot and/or officer in the USSR. As is often the case when peace is established after a period of national upheaval and crisis, there was a tendency to revert to old hierarchies. There was no change in the cultural perception that, except during emergencies, war (and therefore military service) was not women's work.

In July 1945, President Mikhail I. Kalinin spoke to a group of then recently demobilized women soldiers. Although he recognized their strength and bravery, he made no mention of continued military careers; his primary concern was that they find civilian jobs. His closing remarks to them were:

> Equality for women has existed in our country since the very first day of the October Revolution. But you have won equality for women in yet another sphere: in the defense of your country arms in hand. You have won equal rights for women in a field in which they hitherto have not taken such a direct path. But allow me, one grown wise with years, to say to you: do not give yourself airs in your future practical work. Do not talk about the services you rendered, let others do it for you. That will be better.[4]

By his words, Kalinin claimed that the Soviet women veterans had achieved equal rights as soldiers in the war, implying that there would be a role for them to play in the postwar military. Yet Kalinin cautioned that the women should disregard their experiences in combat and let others (presumably men) talk about their accomplishments. It is improbable that such a speech was given to male soldiers returning from the front. Despite their impressive record in combat, the Russian women soldiers were still perceived as short-term solutions rather than full-fledged members of the male-dominated Soviet military. After the war, women were dissuaded in continuing their service in the armed forces.

There appears to have been a deliberate policy in place to downplay the role of Soviet women in combat even before the war ended. In March 1945, Olga Mishakova wrote in *Pravda*, "In the Red Army...women very energetically showed themselves as pilots, snipers, automatic gunners [etc.] ...But they don't forget about their primary duty to nation and state, that of motherhood."[5] No matter how outstanding a woman soldier's performance had been during the war and how badly she was needed in her civilian job, she was reminded by Soviet society that her most important place was in the home.

The rapid demobilization of the women pilots from military service and their virtual exclusion thereafter was largely because of pronatalist governmental policies and the need for workers in the civilian sector. The Soviet Union experienced a significant labor shortage after the war, and homes and families were turned upside down during the five-year conflict. Russia's women were then urged to return to their jobs and homes and create a stable domestic life. Even a year before the war ended, in 1944, awards were given to women who had seven or more children, in an effort to raise the birthrates and encourage adoption.[6] The USSR, crippled by the millions of human lives lost in the war, longed for a return to the relative stability of the prewar days. Women were faced with a dual obligation. While the Soviet government emphasized that women were "first and foremost wives and mothers," they were also workers, and in late 1945, women constituted 63 percent of the workforce in Moscow.[7]

Most of the Soviet women veterans hoped to return to the jobs they held before the war or continue their university education that had been interrupted. Many of the women also had a strong desire to start families, which was typical of women in their early twenties in the 1940s. The war had taken a heavy toll on the women pilots' health, and many of them, who hoped to fly in civil aviation, failed the medical examination. "I had undermined my physical and mental health at the front," remembered pilot Mariya Smirnova. "I was completely exhausted by the four years of war and combat."[8]

In March 1945, the regimental commander of the 46th Guards Aviation Regiment made the decision to send two of its female pilots—Mariya Smirnova and Ekaterina Riabova—to the Zhukovsky Military Aviation Academy in Moscow. Both women were recipients of the prestigious Hero of the Soviet Union medal. When Smirnova and Riabova arrived, they were called into the commanding general's office. Believing that the women's bodies were too weak to study aviation, he recommended they seek other academic pursuits: "You are real heroes of our Motherland. You have already proved what Soviet women are capable of when their help is essential. But the conditions of study in a military academy take a heavy toll on the female body. You lost a lot of strength and health in the war. We must protect you. Enroll to study in a civilian university instead."[9]

It is interesting, although not surprising, that the commanding general used the women's gender to dissuade the two pilots from entering the off-limits male territory of the aviation academy. As Smirnova confirmed above in her own words, the airwomen's health was undermined by the hardships of the war, but despite her apparent handicap, Riabova went on to complete her undergraduate studies, traveled throughout Europe and Asia on speaking engagements, as well as gave birth to a daughter and enrolled in graduate school—only two years after the war. In light of these accomplishments, it is likely that Riabova possessed the necessary strength to have successfully completed her aviation studies at the academy.

A small number of women veterans continued flying in the Air Force for a few years after the war, despite the social pressure to quit their careers in military aviation. "My flying was the best thing I've had in life," said fighter pilot Klavdia Terekhova. Antonina Spitsina Bondareva, a bomber pilot in the 125th Guards Bomber Aviation Regiment, remembered her flying days with affection: "I often have dreams about aircraft—of flying. It is my favorite dream."[10] Like the WASP, a lot of the women pilots married male military pilots or instructors after the war, returned to their homes, and started families. The female veterans, who were interviewed after the war, said although they believed women to be capable of military duty, they were of the opinion that there was no reason for their service in peacetime. Performance, according to historian Reina Pennington, was not the issue, but practicality. In the Soviet Union, military life was particularly arduous, and since Russian men were notorious for rarely doing housework and assisting with childcare, Soviet women found it especially difficult combining family with a military career. Irina Rakobolskaya, chief of staff for the 46th Regiment, saw other opportunities for women who wanted to continue flying after the war. "I think that there is no need for women to serve in military aviation at the present time," she said. "Why would they want to? A passion to fly can be satisfied in sport aviation."[11] Rakobolskaya went on to say, "I think that during the war, when the fate of our country was being decided, the bringing in of women into aviation was justified. But in peacetime a woman can only fly for sport...otherwise how can one combine a career with a family and with maternal happiness?"[12]

War-weariness and the tremendous work involved in rebuilding a nation that had been devastated by war contributed to the reasons the women pilots did not actively protest their exclusion in the postwar military. Nadezhda Popova remembered the suffering that continued in the USSR even after the Nazis had vacated their country: "We came home to face all the destruction and severe food shortages," she said. "We worked eighteen hours a day to reconstruct. Maybe that is why we didn't have much post-combat stress—we didn't have time to reflect on our personal experiences in the war, we were too occupied by the present."[13]

Postwar Soviet women were encouraged to fulfill many roles in the reconstruction of their country. No longer needed for their skills as soldiers, women were then being called back into the workplace and the home. Reina Pennington in her book *Wings, Women, and War,* summed up the three roles the Soviet women pilots were expected to play following World War II:

> Any image of the new Soviet woman as military officer and pilot that resulted from wartime experience was far outweighed by the overwhelming official emphasis on the Soviet woman as mother, wife, and builder of society. Where the Americans had Uncle Sam, the Soviets had Mother Russia. Soviet women were constantly reminded —and many believed—that their true place was on the home front, not the battlefield.[14]

In present day Russia, women are discouraged in seeking combat roles in the armed forces. According to historian Jennifer G. Mathers, "The possibility that women soldiers could serve in combat is almost never mentioned. Combat duty is apparently so obviously not women's work that no one bothers to discuss it."[15] Today Russian servicewomen continue to be viewed by their country as a temporary solution to a current problem and not as equal members of the armed forces.[16] As an increasing number of young Russian men evade conscription in the Russian army, the military has been forced to rely more on its female members. Only a small percentage of women, however, have managed to hold officer rank.

In light of the limited role women are permitted to play in the Russian military today, the achievements of the Soviet airwomen of World War II are that much more significant. One wonders if the pilots of Marina Raskova's 46th Guards Aviation Regiment ever considered the possibility that they would be their country's first—and perhaps last—female military pilots who would be allowed to engage in aerial combat. In the 1960s, a Soviet film titled *Wings* was released with Maya Bulgakova in the starring role. Tatyana Mamonova described the movie's female protagonist: "A heroine —not a beauty—she was a wartime aviator. She had a passion for airplanes, but she was not allowed to indulge in her beloved activity. And so, one day, she took an airplane from the hangar and flew it into the sky."[17]

CONCLUSION

The decade that followed World War II ushered in a robust and prosperous American economy. Even though the United States lost four million female workers in the postwar demobilization,[1] many women who wanted to continue working were able to do so, despite social pressures that encouraged them to return to the home. With the precedent the WASP had set in the 1940s, coupled with favorable economic conditions, it was logical perhaps to presume that women in aviation would move to a new stage of becoming professional pilots. Nothing of the sort happened. The airwomen were excluded from taking part in the emerging postwar field of aviation and seemed to vanish without a trace. Only in the 1970s did women pilots begin to compete with men for professional flying positions.

Jacqueline Cochran, in contrast to the WASP, continued to make headlines after the war. In the summer of 1945, Cochran became the Pacific correspondent for *Liberty* magazine. She witnessed the Japanese surrender in the Philippines, and she was the first American woman inside Japan following V-J Day. Cochran traveled extensively throughout Europe, Asia, and Africa and attended the Nuremberg war-crimes trials in Germany. When she returned to the United States at the end of 1945, she was awarded the Distinguished Service Medal for her contributions during the war. In 1949, Cochran received the French Legion of Honor.

Cochran kept busy with her cosmetics business and began air racing, setting records again. In 1953, with World War II ace and test pilot Chuck Yeager as her coach, she became the first woman to break the sound barrier. Three years later, Cochran made an unsuccessful bid for a congressional seat from California. She campaigned by piloting her own plane around the district. Before Cochran retired in 1970, her longtime ambition was realized when she was promoted to full colonel in the USAF Reserves. She continued flying for many years until a heart condition grounded her. Giving up flying was difficult for Cochran, whose competitive nature pushed her to fly faster and more technically advanced aircraft. America's most accomplished woman pilot passed away at her home in Indio, California, on August 9, 1980. The fearless record-breaking aviator, who had created the first training program for women military pilots in American history, was reportedly buried in a simple pine coffin with her childhood doll. During her memorial service three days later, several jets streaked overhead in a final—albeit unplanned—tribute to a woman who marked her achievements above the clouds. Cochran raised the bar for future generations of airwomen and left an indelible imprint on the history of aviation.

After the Ferry Division's women pilots were demobilized, Nancy Harkness Love finished up her wartime service with another women's aviation first. She went on a flight around the world, during which she was at the controls at least half the way, including the leg going over the Hump—the 20,000-foot-high supply route over the Himalayas that had claimed the lives of 850 airmen during the course of World War II.[2] In July 1946, Nancy and her husband Robert Love became the first couple in history to be decorated at the same time for their military service. Nancy was presented with the Air Medal for her pioneering work with the Ferry Division, and Robert was awarded the Distinguished Service Medal. Love, withdrew to private life, had the first of three daughters in 1947, and stayed active sailing and horseback riding. She continued flying after the war when she and her family moved to Martha's Vineyard, but according to author Marianne Verges, her flying was limited to mostly taking her children to doctor and dentist appointments off-island.[3] Love passed away from cancer on October 22, 1976 in Sarasota, Florida. Despite being overshadowed by the more-visible Jacqueline Cochran, Love is considered by many to be one of the most talented women pilots in American history.

In 1972, a thirtieth anniversary reunion was held in Sweetwater, Texas, and more than 300 WASP, former flight instructors, and Army staff were in attendance. Bruce Arnold, the general's son and a retired Air Force colonel, arrived from Washington, D.C., in place of his father who had been an important advocate for the women pilots during the war. Even Cochran drove into town for the occasion in a fancy mobile home. At this historic reunion the WASP made two important decisions. The first was to promise to get together every two years. The second decision, remarkably more ambitious than the first one, was to right the wrong that had been done to them twenty-eight years earlier and pursue a new militarization bill in Congress. With the women's movement in full swing, and the offer of assistance by Bruce Arnold, who had been a legislative liaison for the Air Force, the former WASP believed that the timing was right for them to finally achieve their goal.

By the mid-1970s, American women were signing up for the all-volunteer armed forces. For the first time in history, women were being admitted to the nation's elite service academies. In September 1976, ten women began training for the USAF and were touted as the "first women military pilots."[4] The WASP, who knew better, were insulted by their country's short-term memory, and they worked even harder to bring their case to Capitol Hill and prove that they had been America's first women military pilots and were deserving of the recognition that accompanied this achievement.

Within a few months an amendment was added to a veterans' bill on the floor of the U.S. Senate that would grant the WASP full military status and make them eligible for veterans' benefits—thirty-two years after they had been deactivated. Senator Barry Goldwater, a former World War II Ferry Division pilot, who had been based at New Castle AAF and had flown with the women ferry pilots, sponsored the bill. It did not take long, however, for veterans' organizations to come out against the amendment, as they did in 1944. Protective of their benefits, they argued that other groups, like the Merchant Marines and the Civil Air Patrol, who also served during the war, might make similar claims to veterans' rights. Collapsing under pressure, the House Veterans' Affairs Committee killed the proposal. Senator Goldwater and Bruce Arnold promised the WASP they would keep up the fight and not give up the battle in Congress.

In March 1977, the WASP bill was reintroduced. This time, every woman member of Congress cosponsored the legislation. The WASP's cause caught the attention of the media, and all across the country WASP circulated petitions and organized letter-writing campaigns. The former women pilots who gathered in Washington, D.C., worked hard to show members of Congress who and what they were, with scrapbooks, correspondences, photos, and official documents saved and treasured for more than thirty years.[5]

Two months later, WASP Dora Doughtery Strother, who after the war earned a doctorate and worked as chief of human factors engineering at Bell Helicopter, testified before the Senate Veterans' Affairs Committee. The testimony Strother gave on May 25, 1977, was reprinted in *Stars and Stripes*. During her talk she outlined for the first time before Congress the history of the entire WASP program, highlighting the arguments that supported militarization. "This is the first time the rank and file members of the WASP have had a chance to tell their story," she said. "We have waited many years for this opportunity."[6] Strother went on to say to the members of Congress: "It is our hope that you, as elected representatives of the people of our country and those in whom our trust lies, will listen to our request with an open heart and open mind, unaffected by the bias and wartime emotions which influenced those in the past who considered our program."[7]

Strother continued to point out the many aspects of the WASP's training as well as flying assignments during the war that were strictly of a military nature. She cited examples such as serving on restricted military bases, having access to military information unknown to civilians, obtaining membership in officer's clubs, and receiving military decorations, which by regulation could not be awarded to civilians.[8] The testimony Strother gave to Congress undoubtedly helped to clear up many misunderstandings that existed about the WASP during World War II.

Despite strong opposition to the WASP bill by the American Legion and the Veterans' Administration, the House passed the WASP amendment to the GI Bill Improvement Act of 1977 on November 3, 1977. The next day the Senate also approved the legislation. For the former airwomen, who had worked hard to be recognized for their achievements during the war, 1977 would be called the year of the WASP. Tears rolled down the cheeks of one WASP watching from the visitors' gallery who had worn her Santiago blue uniform and her silver wings for the historic occasion. Bruce Arnold reportedly reached over and shook her sleeve and told her, "Stop that! You're in uniform," he said, smiling.[9]

According to Marianne Verges in her book *On Silver Wings: The Women Airforce Service Pilots of World War II, 1942–1944*, Arnold may be the individual credited in saving the WASP bill in the eleventh hour. Just before the vote, Arnold was putting together an information packet for the members of Congress, when he discovered in one of the WASP's personal papers a discharge notice that read, "Honorably served in active Federal Service in the Army of the United States."[10] With this official military discharge in hand, Arnold was able to help convince the conservative members of both veterans' committees to support the legislation.

President Jimmy Carter signed the WASP bill into law on Thanksgiving Day, November 23, 1977. On May 21, 1979, thirty-four years after the end of World War II, the USAF offered official recognition by issuing the first honorable discharge to a WASP. Then Assistant Secretary of the Air Force, Antonio Chayes, stated, "The efforts and sacrifices of a talented and courageous group of women have been accorded [retroactive] status as military veterans...and inspire the 47,000 Air Force women who now follow in their footsteps."[11] In 1984, each woman pilot was awarded the Victory medal, and those who had been on active duty for more than a year also received the American Theater medal.

Although grateful for their victory in Congress, there were a few WASP who felt that the benefits they were then afforded under the new militarization law came too late. Barbara Erickson London, who was one of the first WAFS, was not impressed by what the women pilots received in the way of veterans' benefits. "The only thing we can get is a flag on our coffins," she said. "We can go to a military hospital if we're old enough, poor enough, and there's room enough, and we can get, I think $250 for a headstone, and that's about it."[12] London also said she resented the fact that veterans' status was granted to every woman who went through WASP training —even those who washed out and did not graduate. "If a guy went to school and washed out, he was not going to be a veteran," she said. "However, every girl that even went to Sweetwater was on that list. In fact, if you look at this book [WASP roster], if it says trainee after it, those are girls who didn't graduate. That's my only objection."[13]

Former WASP Jean Downey Harman commented on the WASP's legacy in an interview with the author. "The WASP proved that women could do just about anything they set out to do, and that we were really quite capable ...it took the United States a long time to realize that," she said. "Because even getting the veterans' status was like pulling teeth. They had to lump us in with the overseas telephone operators."[14]

Over sixty years after the WASP were released from their World War II flying assignments, the women pilots, many of whom are now grandmothers and great-grandmothers, are still making headlines. An article in the *Washington Post* brought to America's attention the plight of the daughter of deceased WASP Irene Englund, who was told her mother was not entitled to receive military honors or a U.S. flag when her remains were scheduled to be inurned next to those of her husband, also a World War II veteran, at Arlington National Cemetery. Julie Englund, the daughter of the WASP in question, wrote a letter to the editor in the *Post* protesting the situation. After reading her letter, Reginald Brown, then assistant secretary of the Army, whose job was to oversee Arlington National Cemetery, reportedly asked for a review of the rules. It was shocking to discover that almost twenty-five years after the Defense Department implemented the WASP legislation granting them veterans' status, the U.S. Army presumed that the law did not apply to them. On June 1, 2002, the Army announced that they had reconsidered. "This was the most appropriate thing to do to honor these people's services," said Martha Rudd, an Army spokeswoman.[15] Englund, the Army concluded, would be provided "standard honors." Standard honors are provided to enlisted personnel while "full honors" are provided to officers. WASP Irene Englund was interred on June 14, 2002, on Flag Day, and the USAF honor guard conducted the ceremony. The *Washington Post* story that reported on Englund's burial, concluded: "The decision will not allow the WASP and other groups to be buried in the ground at Arlington, which is running low on plots. Instead, the civilians now qualify for inurnment in the cemetery's columbarium complex, which houses cremated remains."[16]

The postwar story of Russian women in military aviation is a relatively short one compared with the accomplishments of today's American female military pilots. The Soviet airwomen's experiences flying in combat were brief, and to date most likely limited to World War II. According to Tina DiGuglielmo in her article "The Role of Women in Soviet Armed Forces: Past, Present, and Future," "The role of women in the Soviet armed forces has been like a pendulum, swinging upward during wartime and back down during peacetime."[17] According to the figures provided by the Soviet

Embassy in 1991, women made up 1 percent of the Soviet military compared with 8.5 percent of women serving that year in the United States.[18] Today there are approximately 100,000 women soldiers in the Russian armed forces, which means that women make up about 10 percent of the total personnel in the Russian military.[19] Men available and fit to be conscripted into the Russian armed forces were estimated to be 21 million in 2006.[20] In comparison, women make up about 14 percent of the U.S. armed forces.[21]

According to research by Jennifer G. Mathers, only 2.9 percent of female soldiers in Russia are commissioned officers. The highest rank women have attained in the Russian military is that of colonel, and fewer than twenty women have reached this position. Women in Russia are not subject to conscription but are eligible to volunteer for the armed forces under the contract service system provided they are aged 19–40, unmarried, and childless.[22]

The largely forgotten achievements of the Soviet women veterans in World War II is an example of what has been called "cultural amnesia" concerning women's military service in Russia today. This is the tendency for national militaries to look upon women as an employment pool to be drawn upon during times of national crisis or when there is a severe shortage of male recruits. When women are needed to fill the ranks, the history of women's military service and performance in previous wars is remembered and even celebrated in order to convince society that women are capable of playing an integral role in the armed forces. Once the fighting is over or the personnel shortage has passed and a sense of normality returns, women are hastily demobilized. The women soldiers' accomplishments in battle are soon forgotten, making any consistent gains for women in the Russian military impossible.[23]

Svetlana Protasova, the first and only woman to fly the Russian Air Force's MiG-29, and a former member of the *Strizhi* ("Swifts") aerobatic team, has defied the odds. Persevering through the strongest opposition to her inclusion in the Russian Air Force, she never gave up on her dream of becoming a fighter pilot. According to Protasova, her future occupation was decided when she was twelve years old after reading Veniamin Kaverin's famous novel *Dva Kapitana* ("Two Captains").[24]

It is not surprising perhaps that following graduation from flight school at Zaporozhye in the Ukraine, and Moscow Aviation Institute, Protasova could not find a job in military aviation. After writing letters to then Russian President Boris Yeltsin and Defense Minister Pavel Grachev, she was referred to the commander of the Russian Air Forces, Army General Pyotr Deynekin who managed to send her to the well-regarded aviation center in Kubinka, a few hours drive from Moscow. Her excitement, however, quickly turned to frustration when instead of being allowed to fly military aircraft, Protasova was kept busy mopping floors and carrying out administrative duties. In the two years she spent in Kubinka, Protasova was not permitted to be lodged on the base with her fellow officers, and she was allowed to fly only once, as a passenger. Fearing that her resignation from the Air Force would only validate her opponents' views that women do not belong in military aviation, Protasova transferred to another air base where she was at last given the opportunity to fly and prove herself as a pilot.[25]

In an interview with London's *Daily Telegraph,* Protasova expressed her feelings about being the only woman fighter pilot in a male-dominated Russian Air Force. "I perform all the exercises—bombing, air combat and interception—no worse than the men. Why shouldn't they consider me their equal?"[26] Protasova, who has been promoted to the rank of captain, is an instructor at the Borisoglebsk Aviation Training Center.

The present status of women pilots in commercial aviation in Russia is not any more promising. According to Nadezhda Kuzhelnaya, a trained cosmonaut, she is only one of two female pilots out of over 1,000 male pilots flying the Tupolev Tu-134 for the Russian airlines, Aeroflot. After being bumped from two Soyuz missions to the International Space Station by "paying customers," Kuzhelnaya resigned from the cosmonaut ranks in 2004.[27] In an interview, Kuzhelnaya remarked, "I believe that more women must be admitted to cosmonauts' training in Russia. Women [are] an important driving force behind human civilization's development. If women can be railroad workers in Russia and lay rails on permanent ways, why could not they fly in space?"[28] If Kuzhelnaya had made it into space, she would have been only the fourth woman cosmonaut in Russia to have done so.

Despite being allies in World War II, the WASP and Soviet women pilots seemed by many to be worlds apart in their ideology, wartime aerial missions, and military status. During the war the airwomen only heard rumors of the other group's existence. Forty-five years after the end of the war, the American and Russian women aviators met face-to-face in a historic reunion in Moscow. The women who were at the 1990 meeting have commented on the strong bonds of sisterhood they experienced with their female counterparts. Even the use of translators did not inhibit their feelings of camaraderie that transcended cultural differences. WASP Anne Noggle interviewed nearly six-dozen Soviet women veterans from 1990 to 1992. As she remarked in the conclusion of her book *A Dance with Death,* "They had gathered as a remembrance, a celebration. They are sisters, they will tell you—closer to one another than to their own relatives. Ultimately their *memento mori* is one of survival, haunted by the ghosts of those not so fortunate."[29]

The dangers and risks inherent in the women pilots' wartime flying assignments, coupled with their patriotic spirit and love of aviation, drew them close together in a way that only individuals who have faced fear and death intimately can know. Gender was the defining factor in both the creation and the dissolution of both groups of airwomen. They suffered discrimination and prejudices from male aircrews and military personnel, and they also earned their respect. The women flyers' very existence in wartime aviation challenged the assumptions of masculine authority and attempted to redefine existing gender boundaries. But as is often the case during a time of war when society is turned on its head, once stability and peace were reestablished, the American and Russian women pilots were told that their services were no longer needed. The return to prewar societal roles was emphasized in both countries, and the aviators who had sacrificed and achieved so much during the conflict were prohibited from taking part in the postwar military.

The accomplishments of women pilots in the 1930s' "Golden Age of Aviation" set an important precedent for the World War II airwomen to follow. Although it took another thirty years for American women to be allowed into the cockpits of military aircraft, and an additional twenty years before they would be allowed to fly in combat, without the achievements of the WASP, it is unlikely that women's presence in modern military aviation would have been assured.

For the Soviet women pilots, their participation in the Great Patriotic War resulted from a way of thinking that persists in Russia today. Perceived as temporary solutions to current problems, Russian servicewomen are not on a par with their male colleagues. Discouraged from seeking combat roles, little evidence exists to show that women military pilots have been given the opportunity to fly in battle since 1945. In modern day Russia, despite its deeply rooted socialist past that boasted gender equality, the idea of women soldiers is an anomaly. According to author Ellen Jones, men in Russia are nurtured in a world dominated by females. She believes that the inclusion of more women in the Russian armed forces may perhaps have a negative effect on the socialization process of males—influencing the male role model and the resultant masculinity of men.[30] Many men in Russia view the military as the last bastion of male superiority in Russia today.

One of the primary things that set the two military cultures apart is opportunity. In the United States armed forces today, women pilots who wish to serve their country are afforded the chance to fly military aircraft and train to become combat fighter pilots. Women aviators in Russia today must overcome tremendous obstacles to be given the same opportunities as their male counterparts. Many of the Soviet women veterans expressed relief when it came time for them to relinquish their flying responsibilities after the war. There were some Russian airwomen however, like many of the WASP, who yearned to keep flying and serving their country. Both groups of skilled pilots were not allowed this possibility for more than three decades following the war.

"This was the best time of our lives," remembered WASP Barbara Erickson London.

We never had a period in our lives that gave us what these three years gave us. We were in the right place at the right time. We were able to fly all of these marvelous airplanes and help with the war which we were very serious about. This experience was probably the greatest experience in our lives for all of us.[31]

In many ways, the experiences of the American and Soviet airwomen in World War II were exactly how one WASP described it: "a magical bubble —a lucky accident in history."[32] The women pilots did not immediately change the course of aviation history nor were they successful in altering the societal norms of their day. But by their courage, professionalism, and determination, the first female military pilots in history, who spread their wings in World War II, succeeded at setting a precedent for subsequent generations of women in aviation.

NOTES

INTRODUCTION

1. Reina Pennington, "The Propaganda Factor and Soviet Women Pilots in World War II," *Minerva: Quarterly Report on Women and the Military* 15, no. 2 (Summer 1997): 13.

2. *The WASPs: Women Pilots of World War II,* radio broadcast. Aired on *All Things Considered,* National Public Radio News, Radio Diaries, 18 December 2002.

3. Svetlana Protasova, the first and only woman to fly the Russian Air Force's MiG-29, is one of Russia's premier female combat fighter pilots in the post–World War II era. It is not known, however, if Protasova has actually been involved in air-to-air combat.

4. Kay Gott, *Women in Pursuit: Flying Fighters for the Air Transport Command Ferrying Division during World War II.* (McKinleyville, California: Kay Gott, 1993), 23–24.

5. D'Ann Campbell, "Women in Combat: The World War II Experience in the United States, Great Britain, Germany and the Soviet Union," *Journal of Military History* 57.2 (April 1993): 301–323.

6. "Germany's 'queen of erotica' dies," *BBC News,* July 18, 2001. [Article online]. http://news.bbc.co.uk/2/hi/europe/1445272.stm (accessed September 27, 2006).

CHAPTER ONE: AMERICA'S FIRST WOMEN MILITARY PILOTS

1. Willam B. Breuer, *War and American Women: Heroism, Deeds and Controversy.* (Westport, Connecticut: Praeger Publishers, 1997), 22.

2. Jacqueline Cochran and Maryann Bucknum Brinley, *Jackie Cochran: The Autobiography of the Greatest Woman Pilot in Aviation History* (New York: Bantam Books, 1987), 15.

3. Amy Nathan, *Yankee Doodle Gals: Women Pilots of World War II* (Washington, D.C.: National Geographic Society, 2001), 17.

4. Sally Van Wagenen Keil, *Those Wonderful Women in Their Flying Machines: The Unknown Heroines of World War II* (New York: Four Directions Press, 1990), 49.

5. Jacqueline Cochran, *The Stars at Noon* (New York: Little Brown, 1954), 41.

6. Nathan, *Yankee Doodle Gals,* 18.

7. Keil, *Those Wonderful Women,* 43.

8. Ann Hodgman and Rudy Djabbaroff, *Sky Stars: The History of Women in Aviation* (New York: Atheneum, 1981), 95–96.

9. Keil, *Those Wonderful Women,* 47.

10. Gott, *Women in Pursuit: Flying Fighters for the Air Transport Command Ferrying Division During World War II* (McKinleyville, California: Kay Gott, 1993), 19.

11. Keil, *Those Wonderful Women,* 50.

12. Cochran, *The Stars at Noon,* 116.

13. Ibid., 51.

14. Cochran and Brinley, *Jackie Cochran: An Autobiography,* 352.

15. Keil, *Those Wonderful Women,* 54.

16. Gott, *Women in Pursuit,* 27.

17. Keil, *Those Wonderful Women,* 119.

18. Marion Stegeman Hodgson, *Winning My Wings: A Woman Airforce Service Pilot in World War II* (Annapolis, Maryland: Naval Institute Press, 1996), 17.

19. Joe Mizrahi, "The WASP Women Airforce Service Pilots," *Airpower* 31, no. 3 (May 2001): 6.

20. Doris Brinker Tanner, "We Also Served," *American History Illustrated* 2, no. 7 (November 1985): 14.

21. Bruce D. Callander, "The WASPs," *Air Force Magazine* 84, no. 4 (April 2001): 4.

22. Mizrahi, "The WASP Women Airforce Service Pilots," 9.

23. John Bollow, "Remembering the WASPs," *Saturday Evening Post* 267, no. 3 (May–June 1995): 58.

24. *Fly Girls,* VHS, produced and directed by Laurel Ladevich (WGBH Educational Foundation, 2000).

25. Ibid.

26. Hodgson, *Winning My Wings,* 28.

27. Juliette Jenner Stege, interview by the author, September 8, 2006.

28. Ibid.

29. Mizrahi, "The WASPs Women Airforce Service Pilots," 20.

30. Tanner, "We Also Served," 16.

31. Adaline Blank, *Women Airforce Service Pilots. Correspondence July 1943–December 1943,* (Denton, Texas: Texas Woman's University Archives, The Woman's Collection, 2002).

32. Florence G. Shutsy-Reynolds, interview by the author, September 8, 2006.

33. Jean Hascall Cole, *Women Pilots of World War II* (Salt Lake City, Utah: University of Utah Press, 1992), 33.

34. Nathan, *Yankee Doodle Gals,* 46.

35. Ibid., 9.

36. Mizrahi, "The WASP Women Airforce Service Pilots," 2.

37. General Paul Tibbets, *Women Airforce Service Pilots: An Oral History* (Denton, Texas: Texas Woman's University Archives, The Woman's Collection, 2002).

38. *Fly Girls.*

39. Molly Merryman, *Clipped Wings: The Rise and Fall of the Women Airforce Service Pilots (WASPs) of World War II* (New York: New York University Press, 1998). 101.

40. *Fly Girls.*

41. Susan M. Hartmann, *The Home Front and Beyond: American Women in the 1940s* (Boston, Massachusetts: Twayne Publishers, 1982), 1.

42. Ibid., 16.

43. Ibid., 17.

44. Ibid., 21.

45. Karen L. Anderson, *Wartime Women: Sex Roles, Family Relations, and the Status of Women During World War II* (Westport, Connecticut: Greenwood Publishing Group, 1981), 63.

46. Tanner, "We Also Served," 49.

47. Ibid., 4.

CHAPTER TWO: MARINA RASKOVA AND HER SOVIET AVIATION REGIMENTS

1. Helene Keyssar and Vladimir Pozner, *Remembering War: A U.S.–Soviet Dialogue* (New York: Oxford University Press, 1990), 39–40; interview with Yevgeniya Zhigulenko.

2. Kazimiera J. Cottam, *Women in War and Resistance: Selected Biographies of Soviet Women Soldiers* (Nepean, Canada: New Military Publishing, 1998), 18.

3. Ibid., 20.

4. Ibid.

5. Ibid., 21.

6. Ibid., 22.

7. Anne Noggle, *A Dance with Death: Soviet Airwomen in World War II* (College Station, Texas: Texas A&M University Press, 1994), 15.

8. Reina Pennington, *Wings, Women, and War: Soviet Airwomen in World War II Combat* (Lawrence, Kansas: University Press of Kansas, 2001), 17.

9. David L. Hoffmann, *Stalinist Values: The Cultural Norms of Soviet Modernity 1917–1941* (Ithaca, New York: Cornell University Press, 2003), 113.

10. Pennington, *Wings, Women, and War,* 19.

11. Ibid., 23.

12. Ibid., 26.

13. Amy Goodpaster Strebe, "Marina Raskova and the Soviet Women Aviators of World War II," *Russian Life* 46, no. 1 (January/February 2003): 46.

14. On June 18, 2005, Galina Brok-Beltsova, along with Anna I. Kirilina, armament mechanic in the 125th Guards (587th) Bomber Aviation Regiment, and Ekaterina K. Polunina, senior aircraft mechanic in the 586th Fighter Aviation Regiment, traveled to the United States to be honored at the San Diego Aerospace Museum.

15. Phyllis Anne Duncan, "How They Must Love Their Homeland," *FAA Aviation News*, May/June 2002, 21.

16. Kazimiera J. Cottam, *Women in Air War: The Eastern Front of World War II* (Nepean, Canada: New Military Publishing, 1997), xvii.

17. Bruce Myles, *Night Witches: The Untold Story of Soviet Women in Combat* (Chicago, Illinois: Academy Chicago Publishers, 1981), 270.

18. Mary Buckley, "Complex 'Realities' of 'New' Women of the 1930s: Assertive, Superior, Belittled and Beaten," in *Gender in Russian History and Culture,* ed. Linda Edmondson (New York: Palgrave, 2001), 180.

19. Lynne Attwood, "Rationality Versus Romanticism: Representations of Women in the Stalinist Press," in *Gender in Russian History and Culture,* ed. Linda Edmondson (New York: Palgrave, 2001), 161.

20. Ibid.

21. Richard Stites, *The Women's Liberation Movement in Russia: Feminism, Nihilism, and Bolshevism 1860–1930* (Princeton, New Jersey: Princeton University Press, 1990), 395.

22. Susan M. Hartmann, *The Home Front and Beyond: American Women in the 1940s* (Boston, Massachusetts: Twayne Publishers, 1982), 21.

23. Barbara Evans Clements, "Later Developments: Trends in Soviet Women's History, 1930 to the Present," in *Russia's Women: Accommodation, Resistance, Transformation,* ed. Barbara Evans Clements, Barbara Alpern Engel, and Christine D. Worobec. (Berkeley, California: University of California Press, 1991), 272.

24. Stites, *The Women's Liberation Movement in Russia,* 429.

25. Vicki L. Friedl, *Women in the U.S. Military, 1901–1995: A Research Guide and Annotated Bibliography* (Westport, Connecticut: Greenwood Publishing Group, 1996), 12.

26. Noggle, *A Dance with Death,* 6.

27. Pennington, *Wings, Women, and War,* 8.

28. Ibid., 8.

29. Ibid., 9.

30. Ibid., 10.

31. Ibid., 9.

32. Noggle, *A Dance with Death,* 10–11.

33. Pennington, *Wings, Women, and War,* 35.

34. Raisa E. Aronova, *Nochnye ved'my* [Night Witches] (Moscow: Sovetskaia Rossiia, 1969), 24.

35. Pennington, *Wings, Women, and War,* 39.

36. Aronova, *Nochnye ved'my* [Night Witches], 28.

37. Shelley Saywell, *Women in War* (Markham, Ontario, Canada: Penguin Books Canada Ltd., 1985), 138.

38. Ibid.

39. Pennington, *Wings, Women, and War*, 37.

40. Ibid., 42.

41. Saywell, *Women in War*, 138.

42. Pennington, *Wings, Women, and War*, 45.

43. *The Night Witches: Soviet Air Women in World War II*, Documentary film, produced and directed by Sissi Hüetlin and Elizabeth McKay (London: Move A Mountain Productions, 1994).

44. Strebe, "Marina Raskova and the Soviet Women Aviators of World War II," 47.

45. Cottam, *Women in War and Resistance*, 27.

46. Duncan, "How They Must Have Loved Their Homeland."

47. Cottam, *Women in War and Resistance*, 25.

48. Pennington, *Wings, Women, and War*, 49.

49. Saywell, *Women in War*, 139.

50. *The Night Witches*, Documentary film, 1994.

51. Vladimir Belyakov, "Russia's Women Top Guns," *Aviation History*, March 2000, 36.

52. Ekaterina K. Polunina, *Devchonki, podruzhki, letchitsy* [Girls, girlfriends, pilots] (Moscow: Izdatel'sky Dom "Vestnik Vozdushnogo Flota," 2004), 146.

53. Ibid., 139.

54. Pennington, *Wings, Women, and War*, 142.

CHAPTER THREE: PATRIOTISM AND A LOVE OF FLYING

1. Nathan, *Yankee Doodle Gals*, 46.

2. Hartmann, *The Home Front and Beyond: American Women in the 1940s*, 31–32.

3. Dale R. Herspring, "Women in the Russian Military: A Reluctant Marriage," *Minerva: Quarterly Report on Women and the Military* 15, no. 2 (Summer 1997): 44.

4. Linda Grant De Pauw, *Battle Cries and Lullabies: Women in War from Prehistory to the Present* (Norman, Oklahoma: University of Oklahoma Press, 1998), 215.

5. Pennington, *Wings, Women, and War*, 8.

6. Ibid.

7. Leila Rupp, *Mobilizing Women for War: German and American Propaganda, 1939–1945* (Princeton, New Jersey: Princeton University Press, 1978), 96.

8. Maureen Honey, *Creating Rosie the Riveter: Class, Gender, and Propaganda during World War II*(Amherst, Massachusetts: The University of Massachusetts Press, 1984), 40–41.

9. Clements, "Later Developments," 272.

10. Lisa A. Kirschenbaum, "Our City, Our Hearths, Our Families: Local Loyalties and Private Life in Soviet World War II Propaganda," *Slavic Review* 59, no. 4 (Winter 2000): 825.

11. Hartmann, *The Home Front and Beyond: American Women in the 1940s*, 42.

12. Anne Noggle, *For God, Country and the Thrill of It: Women Airforce Service Pilots in World War II* (College Station, Texas: Texas A&M University Press, 1990), 12.

13. Ibid.

14. Cornelia Fort, "At Twilight's Last Gleaming," *Woman's Home Companion*, July 1943, 19.

15. Ibid.

16. Tanner, "We Also Served," 19.

17. Hodgson, *Winning My Wings*, 26.

18. *The WASPs: Women Pilots of World War II*.

19. Marianne Verges, *On Silver Wings: The Women Airforce Service Pilots of World War II 1942–1944* (New York: Ballantine Books, 1991), 237.

20. *Fly Girls*.

21. Ann Baumgartner Carl, *A WASP Among Eagles: A Woman Military Test Pilot in World War II* (Washington, D.C.: Smithsonian Press, 1999), 25.

22. Ibid., 28.

23. Cole, *Women Pilots of World War II*, 7.

24. Pennington, *Wings, Women, and War*, 169.

25. Ibid., 170.

26. Kazimiera J. Cottam, *In the Sky Above the Front: A Collection of Memoirs of Soviet Air Women Participants in the Great Patriotic War* (Manhattan, Kansas: Sunflower University Press, 1984), 194.

27. Saywell, *Women in War*, 137–138.

28. Noggle, *A Dance with Death*, 80.

29. Saywell, *Women in War*, 137.

30. Cottam, *Women in War and Resistance*, 12.

CHAPTER FOUR: GENDER ISSUES

1. Cole, *Women Pilots of World War II*, 138.

2. *Women of Courage: The Story of the Women Pilots of World War II*, Documentary film, 1993.

3. Keil, *Those Wonderful Women*, 129.

4. Ibid.

5. Janet Goetze, "And now, the last of the first: The U.S. military's earliest women pilots reunite for a convention in Portland," *The Oregonian*, September 9, 2006, C6.

6. Keil, *Those Wonderful Women*, 257.

7. *Fly Girls*.

8. Hodgson, *Winning My Wings*, 24.

9. Callander, "The WASPs," 6.

10. Jean Downey Harman, interview by the author, August 24, 2001.

11. Ibid.

12. Nathan, *Yankee Doodle Gals*, 52.

13. Bollow, "Remembering the WASPs," 60.

14. Marion Schorr Brown, *Women Airforce Service Pilots: An Oral History* (Denton, Texas: Texas Woman's University Archives, The Woman's Collection, 2002), 36.

15. Cochran and Brinley, *Jackie Cochran*, 20.

16. Nathan, *Yankee Doodle Gals*, 57.

17. Luanne C. Lea, "Women, Aviation and the Media," *Women in Aviation* 3 (January–February 1992): 3.

18. "Girl Pilots: Air Force Trains Them at Avenger Field, Texas," *Life*, July 19, 1943, 80.

19. Dean Jaros, *Heroes Without Legacy: American Airwomen, 1912–1944* (Boulder, Colorado: University Press of Colorado, 1993), 106.

20. Nathan, *Yankee Doodle Gals*, 77.

21. *WASPs and Witches: The History of Women Pilots Fighting for the Right to Fight*, DVD, produced and directed by Jamie Doran (Atlantic Celtic Films, 2000).

22. Ibid.

23. *Zhenshchiny na za Shchite Otechestva 1941–1945* [Women in Defense of the Fatherland 1941–1945], vol. 3 (Moscow: Russian Committee of Veterans of the War, 2000), 188–189.

24. Ibid.

25. Cottam, *Women in Air War*, 109.

26. Noggle, *A Dance with Death*, 111.

27. Reina Pennington, "'Do Not Speak of the Services You Rendered': Women Veterans of Aviation in the Soviet Union," *Journal of Slavic Military Studies* 9, no. 1 (March 1996): 120–151; reprinted in *A Soldier and A Woman: Sexual Integration in the Military*, ed.Gerald J. DeGroot and Corinna Peniston-Bird (London: Longman, 2000), 156.

28. Ibid.

29. Ibid.

30. Noggle, *A Dance with Death*, 105.

31. Pennington, *Wings, Women, and War*, 44.

32. Noggle, *A Dance with Death*, 86.

33. Ibid., 47.

34. Saywell, *Women in War*, 144.

35. Robyn Dixon, "Women of War: 'Night Witches' Recall Fighting Nazi Invaders With Suicidal Courage," *Los Angeles Times*, May 20, 2001, 4AA.

36. For a more detailed account of Anna Timofeeva-Egorova's combat experiences in the war, see Anna Timofeeva-Egorova, "Derzhis' Sestrenka!" [Hold Fast, Sister!] *Voenno-Istoricheskii Zhurnal* (USSR) 3 (1983): 68–74.

37. Noggle, *A Dance with Death*, 37.

38. Saywell, *Women in War*, 149.

39. Noggle, *A Dance with Death*, 94.

40. Saywell, *Women in War*, 145.

41. Noggle, *A Dance with Death*, 56.

42. Saywell, *Women in War*, 145.

43. Pennington, "Do Not Speak of the Services You Rendered," 161–162.

44. Pennington, "The Propaganda Factor," 26.

45. Barbara Evans Clements, Barbara Alpern Engel, and Christine D. Worobec, eds., *Russia's Women: Accommodation, Resistance, Transformation* (Berkeley, California: University of California Press, 1991), 12–13.

CHAPTER FIVE: THE TIES THAT BIND

1. Noggle, *A Dance with Death*, 85.

2. Anne Noggle, "Return of the WASPs," *Air & Space*, June/July 1990, 87.

3. Harman interview.

4. Shutsy-Reynolds interview.

5. Ibid.

6. Carl, *A WASP Among Eagles*, 49.

7. Ibid.

8. Noggle, "Return of the WASPs," 84.

9. Nathan, *Yankee Doodle Gals*, 58.

10. *Fly Girls.*

11. Ibid.

12. Keil, *Those Wonderful Women*, 227–228.

13. Ibid., 232.

14. Saywell, *Women in War*, 144.

15. Pennington, *Wings, Women, and War*, 169.

16. Noggle, *A Dance with Death*, 12.

17. Ibid., 46.

18. Ibid., 34.

19. *The Night Witches: Soviet Air Women in World War II*, Documentary film, 1994.

20. Noggle, *A Dance with Death*, 47.

21. Ibid., 59.

22. Cottam, *Women in Air War*, 190.

23. For a personal account of the 46th Guards Aviation Regiment's wartime missions and conditions at the front, see Yevgeniya Maksimova Rudneva and Irina V. Rakobolskaya, eds., *Poka stuchit serdtse: dnevnik I pis'ma geroia Sovetskogo Soiuza Evgenii Rudnevoi* [As Long as the Heart Beats: The Diary and Letters of the Hero of the Soviet Union Yevgeniya Rudneva], (Moscow: Izdatel'stvo Moskovskgo Universiteta, 1995).

24. Natalia Rybalkina, "A Visit to the 'Night Witches,'" *Soviet Woman*, November 1990, 5.

25. Hodgson, *Winning My Wings*, 256.

26. Noggle, *A Dance with Death*, x.

CHAPTER SIX: THE WASP ARE DISBANDED

1. Quote is from an interview by Nancy Parrish with WASP Annelle Henderson Bulechek on the official WASP website. (http://www.wasp-wwii.org/wasp/home.htm) (accessed September 28, 2006).

2. Merryman, *Clipped Wings,* 33.

3. Ibid., 28.

4. *Fly Girls.*

5. Merryman, *Clipped Wings,* 42.

6. John O'Donnell, "Capitol Stuff," *Washington Times Herald,* March 31, 1944.

7. "Army Passes Up Jobless Pilots to Train Wasps: Prefers Women to Older, Experienced Flyers," *Chicago Tribune Press Service,* February 11, 1944.

8. "WASPs to Be Part of Army Under War Department Plan," Associated Press, 4 May 1944.

9. Merryman, *Clipped Wings,* 66.

10. Byrd Howell Granger, *On Final Approach: The Women Airforce Service Pilots of WWII* (Scottsdale, Arizona: Falconer Publishing Co., 1991), 392–393.

11. "WASPs to Get Snappy Outfits Costing $505," *Washington, D.C. Star,* June 10, 1944.

12. Granger, *On Final Approach,* A-90/E.

13. Merryman, *Clipped Wings,* 80.

14. Ibid., 81.

15. Ibid., 82.

16. Congressional Record—Appendix, June 17, 1944, A3344. (Denton, Texas: Texas Woman's University Archives, The Woman's Collection).

17. Keil, *Those Wonderful Women,* 303.

18. Merryman, *Clipped Wings,* 103.

19. Ibid.

20. "Voices From On High," (editorial on the WASP), *Contact,* October 1944, 16.

21. Ibid.

22. Ibid.

23. Merryman, *Clipped Wings,* 174.

24. Ibid., 180.

25. Nathan, *Yankee Doodle Gals,* 78.

26. *Women of Courage: The Story of the Women Pilots of World War II.*

27. Harman interview.

28. Cole, *Women Pilots of World War II,* 135.

29. Keil, *Those Wonderful Women,* 331.

30. Dora Dougherty Strother, "The WASP Training Program," *Journal of American Aviation Historical Society* 19, no. 4 (4th Quarter 1974): 306.

31. Tanner, "We Also Served," 47.

32. Keil, *Those Wonderful Women,* 332–333.

33. Shutsy-Reynolds interview.

34. Keil, *Those Wonderful Women,* 322.

35. Nathan, *Yankee Doodle Gals,* 78.

36. Harman interview.

37. Melissa Domsic, "Portraits of Perseverance: Exhibit honors roles of women in military," *The San Diego Union-Tribune,* September 11, 2006, B3.

38. Noggle, *For God, Country, and the Thrill of It,* 14.

39. Shutsy-Reynolds interview.

40. *Women of Courage: The Story of the Women Pilots of World War II.*

41. Cole, *Women Pilots of World War II,* 136.

CHAPTER SEVEN: DEMOBILIZATION OF THE SOVIET AIRWOMEN

1. Noggle, *A Dance with Death,* 145.

2. Vladimir Karpov, *Russia at War 1941–1945* (New York: The Vendome Press, 1987), 230–231.

3. Anne Eliot Griesse and Richard Stites, "Russia: Revolution and War," in *Female Soldiers—Combatants or Noncombatants?: Historical and Contemporary Perspectives,* ed. Nancy Loring Goldman (Westport, Connecticut: Greenwood Publishing Group, 1982), 78.

4. M.I. Kalinin, *On Communist Education: Selected Speeches and Articles* (Moscow: Foreign Languages Publishing House, 1953), 428.

5. Pennington, "The Propaganda Factor," 31.

6. Kirschenbaum, "Our City, Our Hearths, Our Families: Local Loyalties and Private Life in Soviet World War II Propaganda," 846.

7. Gregory Malloy Smith, "The Impact of World War II on Women, Family Life, and Mores in Moscow, 1941–1945" (Ph.D. diss., Stanford University, 1989), 333.

8. Noggle, *A Dance with Death,* 37.

9. Pennington, "Do Not Speak of the Services You Rendered," 168.

10. Noggle, *A Dance with Death,* 109.

11. Pennington, "Do Not Speak of the Services You Rendered," 164.

12. Ibid., 166.

13. Saywell, *Women in War,* 157.

14. Pennington, *Wings, Women, and War,* 174–175.

15. Jennifer G. Mathers, "Women in the Russian Armed Forces: A Marriage of Convenience?" *Minerva: Quarterly Report on Women and the Military* 18, nos. 3–4 (Fall/Winter 2000): 138.

16. Herspring, "Women in the Russian Military: A Reluctant Marriage," 53.

17. Tatyana Mamonova, *Russian Women's Studies: Essays on Sexism in Soviet Russia* (New York: Pergamon Press, 1989), 150.

CONCLUSION

1. Jaros, *Heroes Without Legacy,* 119.

2. Verges, *On Silver Wings,* 229.

3. Ibid.

4. Ibid., 232.

5. Ibid., 234.

6. "Dora Dougherty Strother Testifies For WASPs Veterans' Status," *Stars and Stripes,* June 2, 1977, 3.

7. Ibid.

8. Ibid., 6.

9. Verges, *On Silver Wings,* 236.

10. Ibid.

11. Tanner, "We Also Served," 49.

12. Gail M. Gutierrez, *Forgotten Wings: An Oral History of Women Airforce Service Pilots, the WASPs* (Fullerton, California: Oral History Project, California State University, Fullerton, 1992), 101.

13. Ibid.

14. Harman interview.

15. Steve Vogel, "Civilians Allowed Military Honors at Arlington," *Washington Post,* June 1, 2002, A09.

16. Ibid.

17. Tina DiGuglielmo, "The Role of Women in the Soviet Armed Forces: Past, Present and Future," in *Beyond Glasnost: Soviet Reform and Security Issues,* ed. David Thomas Twining (Westport, Connecticut: Greenwood Publishing Group, 1992), 40.

18. Ibid., 52.

19. Jennifer G. Mathers, "Women, Society and the Military: Women Soldiers in Post-Soviet Russia," in *Military and Society in Post-Soviet Russia,* ed. Stephen L. Webber and Jennifer G. Mathers (Manchester: University of Manchester Press, 2006), 207.

20. CIA World Fact Book 2006, https://www.cia.gov/cia/publications/factbook/geos/rs.html#Military (accessed November 9, 2006).

21. Mathers, "Women, Society and the Military: Women Soldiers in Post-Soviet Russia," 208.

22. Ibid., 211.

23. Ibid., 214–215.

24. *Russian Women Aviators: A Panel Discussion,* featuring Nadezhda Kuzhel-naya, Svetlana Protasova, and Lidiya Zaitseva, VHS (Seattle, Washington, The Museum of Flight, March 18, 2006).

25. Sergei Babichev, "A Woman's Affair (Russian Pilot Svetlana Protasova)," *Russian Life,* March 1997, 9–12.

26. Marcus Warren, "MiG Pilot Flies in Face of Russian Male Prejudice," *Daily Telegraph,* 1504, (July 8, 1999) http://www.telegraph.co.uk/htmlContent.jhtml?html=/archive/1999/07/08/wpil08.html (accessed September 17, 2006).

27. *Russian Women Aviators: A Panel Discussion.*

28. Yuri Karash, "Training of a Female Cosmonaut." *Space.com* (January 26, 2001) [Article online] http://www.space.com/news/spaceagencies/woman_cosmonaut_010126.html. (accessed September 17, 2006).

29. Noggle, *A Dance with Death*, 317.

30. Ellen Jones, *Red Army and Society: Sociology of the Soviet Military* (Boston, Massachusetts: Allen & Unwin, 1985), 103.

31. *Women of Courage: The Story of the Women Pilots of World War II.*

32. *The WASPs: Women Pilots of World War II.*

BIBLIOGRAPHY

SPECIFIC WORKS ON WOMEN AIRFORCE SERVICE PILOTS (WASP)

"Army Passes Up Jobless Pilots to Train Wasps: Prefers Women to Older, Experienced Flyers," Chicago Tribune Press Service, February 11, 1944.

Blank, Adaline. *Women Airforce Service Pilots. Correspondence July 1943–December 1943*. Denton, Texas: Texas Woman's University Archives, The Woman's Collection, 2002.

Bollow, John. "Remembering the WASPs." *Saturday Evening Post* 267, no. 3 (May–June 1995): 58–63.

Brown, Marion Schorr. *Women Airforce Service Pilots: An Oral History*. Denton, Texas: Texas Woman's University Archives, The Woman's Collection, 2002.

Callander, Bruce D. "The WASPs." *Air Force Magazine* 84, no. 4 (April 2001): 1–7.

Carl, Ann Baumgartner. *A WASP Among Eagles: A Woman Military Test Pilot in World War II*. Washington, D.C.: Smithsonian Press, 1999.

Clayton, Sylvia Dahmes. *Women Airforce Service Pilots: An Oral History*. Denton, Texas: Texas Woman's University Archives, The Woman's Collection, 2002.

Cochran, Jacqueline, and Maryann Bucknum Brinley. *Jackie Cochran: The Autobiography of the Greatest Woman Pilot in Aviation History*. New York: Bantam Books, 1987.

Cochran, Jacqueline. *The Stars at Noon*. New York: Little Brown, 1954.

Cole, Jean H. *Women Pilots of World War II*. Salt Lake City: University of Utah Press, 1992.

Congressional Record—Appendix, 17 June 1944, A3344. Denton, Texas: Texas Woman's University Archives, The Woman's Collection.

Domsic, Melissa. "Portraits of Perseverance: Exhibit Honors Roles of Women in Military." *The San Diego Union-Tribune,* September 11, 2006, B1 and B3.

Donnelly, Karen. *American Women Pilots of World War II.* New York: The Rosen Publishing Group, Inc., 2004.

"Dora Dougherty Strother Testifies For WASPs Veterans' Status." *Stars and Stripes* (June 2, 1977): 3, 6, 9.

Drake, Helan Kelly. *Memories of Other Times and Places: One Little Girl's Impression of WASP Trainees.* WASP WWII Stores, 1992.

Fly Girls. VHS. Produced and directed by Laurel Ladevich. 60 min. Boston, Massachusetts: WGBH Educational Foundation, 2000.

Fort, Cornelia. "At Twilight's Last Gleaming." *Woman's Home Companion,* July 1943, 19.

"Girl Pilots: Air Force Trains Them at Avenger Field, Texas." *Life,* July 19, 1943, 73–81.

Goetze, Janet. "And Now, the Last of the First: The U.S. Military's Earliest Women Pilots Reunite for a Convention in Portland." *The Oregonian,* September 9, 2006, C1 and C6.

Gott, Kay. *Women in Pursuit: Flying Fighters for the Air Transport Command Ferrying Division during World War II.* McKinleyville, California: Kay Gott, 1993.

Granger, Byrd Howell. *On Final Approach: The Women Airforce Service Pilots of WWII.* Scottsdale, Arizona: Falconer Publishing Co., 1991.

Gutierrez, Gail M. *Forgotten Wings: An Oral History of Women Airforce Service Pilots, the WASPs.* Fullerton, California: Oral History Project, California State University, Fullerton, 1992.

Harman, Jean Downey, Women Airforce Service Pilot. Interview with the author, August 24, 2001.

Hodgson, Marion Stegeman. *Winning My Wings: A Woman Airforce Service Pilot in World War II.* Annapolis, Maryland: Naval Institute Press, 1996.

Keil, Sally Van Wagenen. *Those Wonderful Women in Their Flying Machines: The Unknown Heroines of World War II.* New York: Four Directions Press, 1990.

Langley, Wanda. *Flying Higher: The Women Airforce Service Pilots of World War II.* North Haven, Connecticut: The Shoe String Press, Inc., 2002.

Merl, Jean. "Aviation Buff Hopes to Discover Fate of Female War Pilot Who Vanished After Takeoff in 1944." *Los Angeles Times,* September 14, 1997, B14 and B17.

Merryman, Molly. *Clipped Wings: The Rise and Fall of the Women Airforce Service Pilots (WASPs) of World War II.* New York: New York University Press, 1998.

Meyer, Norma. "Female Pilot Missing Since '44 Target of Searchers' Expedition." *The San Diego Union-Tribune,* August 12, 2001, A3–A4.

Minton, Madge Rutherford. *Women Airforce Service Pilots, Class of 43-W-4: Letters 1943–1944.* Denton, Texas: Texas Woman's University Archives, The Woman's Collection, 1998.

Mizrahi, Joe. "The WASP Women Airforce Service Pilots." *Airpower* 31, no. 3, (May 2001): 1–35.

Moore, Madge Ragan Leon. *Women Airforce Service Pilots: An Oral History.* Denton, Texas: Texas Woman's University, The Woman's Collection, 2002.

Nathan, Amy. *Yankee Doodle Gals: Women Pilots of World War II.* Washington, D.C.: National Geographic Society, 2001.

Noggle, Anne. *For God, Country and the Thrill of It: Women Airforce Service Pilots in World War II.* College Station, Texas: Texas A&M University Press, 1990.

———. "Return of the WASPs." *Air & Space,* June/July 1990,: 82–87.

O'Donnell, John. "Capitol Stuff," *Washington Times Herald,* March 31, 1944.

Shutsy-Reynolds, Florence G., Women Airforce Service Pilot. Interview with the author, September 8, 2006.

Stege, Juliette Jenner, Women Airforce Service Pilot. Interview with the author, September 8, 2006.

Strother, Dora Dougherty. "The WASP Training Program." *Journal of American Aviation Historical Society* 19, no. 4 (4th Quarter 1974): 298–306.

Tanner, Doris Brinker. "We Also Served." *American History Illustrated* 2, no. 7 (1985): 12–21, 47–49.

Tibbets, General Paul. *Women Airforce Service Pilots: An Oral History.* Denton, Texas: Texas Woman's University Archives, The Woman's Collection, 2002.

Verges, Marianne. *On Silver Wings: The Women Airforce Service Pilots of World War II, 1942–1944.* New York: Ballantine Books, 1991.

Vogel, Steve. "Civilians Allowed Military Honors at Arlington." *Washington Post,* June 1, 2002, A09.

"Voices From On High," (editorial on the WASPs). *Contact,* October 1944, 16.

"WASPs to Be Part of Army under War Department Plan," Associated Press, May 4, 1944.

The WASPs: Women Pilots of World War II. Radio broadcast. Produced by Joe Richman. Aired on *All Things Considered* National Public Radio News, Radio Diaries, December 18, 2002.

Winston, Sara Chapin. *Women Airforce Service Pilots: An Oral History.* Denton, Texas: Texas Woman's University Archives, The Woman's Collection, 1996.

Women of Courage: The Story of the Women Pilots of World War II. VHS. Produced and directed by Ken Magid. Lakewood, Colorado: K.M. Productions, Inc., 1993.

Wyall, Mary Anna Martin. *Women Airforce Service Pilots, Class of 44-W-10: Letters 1944–1945.* Denton, Texas: Texas Woman's University Archives, The Woman's Collection, 1998.

GENERAL WORKS ON WOMEN IN AVIATION/MILITARY/ SOCIETY/WAR—UNITED STATES

Adams, Jean, and Margaret Kimball. *Heroines of the Sky.* Garden City, New York: The Junior Literary Guild and Doubleday, Doran & Company, Inc., 1942.

Addis, Elisabetta, Valeria E. Russo, and Lorenza Sebesta, eds. *Women Soldiers: Images and Realities.* New York: St. Martin's Press, 1994.

Anderson, Karen L. *Wartime Women: Sex Roles, Family Relations, and the Status of Women During World War II.* Westport, Connecticut: Greenwood Publishing Group, 1981.

Boase, Wendy. *The Sky's the Limit: Women Pioneers in Aviation.* New York: Macmillan Publishing, Co., Inc., 1979.

Breuer, Willam B. *War and American Women: Heroism, Deeds and Controversy.* Westport, Connecticut: Praeger Publishers, 1997.

Chafe, William H. *The American Woman: Her Changing Social, Economic and Political Roles, 1920–1970.* New York: Oxford University Press, 1972.

———. *The Paradox of Change: American Women in the 20th Century.* New York: Oxford University Press, 1991.

Degroot, Gerard J., and Corinna Peniston-Bird, eds. *A Soldier and a Woman: Sexual Integration in the Military.* London: Longman, 2000.

De Pauw, Linda Grant. *Battle Cries and Lullabies: Women in War from Prehistory to the Present.* Norman, Oklahoma: University of Oklahoma Press, 1998.

Friedl, Vicki L. *Women in the U.S. Military, 1901–1995: A Research Guide and Annotated Bibliography.* Westport, Connecticut: Greenwood Publishing Group, 1996.

Goldman, Nancy Loring, ed. *Female Soldiers—Combatants or Noncombatants?: Historical and Contemporary Perspectives.* Westport, Connecticut: Greenwood Press, 1982.

Hartmann, Susan M. *The Home Front and Beyond: American Women in the 1940s.* Boston, Massachusetts: Twayne Publishers, 1982.

Haynsworth, Leslie, and David Toomey. *Amelia Earhart's Daughters: The Wild and Glorious Story of American Women Aviators from World War II to the Dawn of the Space Age.* New York: William Morrow and Company, Inc., 1998.

Higonnet, Margaret Randolph, Jane Jenson, Sonya Michel, and Margaret Collins Weitz, eds. *Behind the Lines: Gender and the Two World Wars.* New Haven, Connecticut: Yale University Press, 1987.

Hodgman, Ann, and Rudy Djabbaroff. *Sky Stars: The History of Women in Aviation.* New York: Atheneum, 1981.

Honey, Maureen. *Creating Rosie the Riveter: Class, Gender, and Propaganda During World War II.* Amherst, Massachusetts: The University of Massachusetts Press, 1984.

Jaros, Dean. *Heroes Without Legacy: American Airwomen, 1912–1944.* Boulder, Colorado: University Press of Colorado, 1993.

Lea, Luanne C. "Women, Aviation and the Media." *Women in Aviation* 3 (January–February 1992): 3–4.

Lebow, Eileen F. *Before Amelia: Women Pilots in the Early Days of Aviation.* Washington, D.C.: Brassey's, Inc., 2002.

Lomax, Judy. *Women of the Air.* New York: Dodd, Mead & Company, 1987.

Milkman, Ruth. *Gender at Work: The Dynamics of Job Segregation by Sex During World War II.* Chicago, Illinois: University of Illinois Press, 1987.

Nathan, Amy. *Count On Us: American Women in the Military.* Washington, D.C.: National Geographic Society, 2004.

Peckham, Betty. *Women in Aviation*. New York: Thomas Nelson & Sons, 1945.

Rupp, Leila. *Mobilizing Women for War: German and American Propaganda, 1939–1945*. Princeton, New Jersey: Princeton University Press, 1978.

Smith, Elizabeth Simpson. *Breakthrough: Women in Aviation*. New York: Walker and Company, 1981.

———. *Coming Out Right: The Story of Jacqueline Cochran, the First Woman Aviator to Break the Sound Barrier*. New York: Walker and Company, 1991.

Stiehm, Judith Hicks, ed. *It's Our Military, Too! Women and the U.S. Military*. Philadelphia, Pennsylvania: Temple University Press, 1996.

Women Combat Pilots: The Right Stuff. DVD. The History Channel. A&E Television Networks, 2003.

Zeinert, Karen. *Those Incredible Women of World War II*. Brookfield, Connecticut: The Millbrook Press, 1994.

SPECIFIC WORKS ON SOVIET WOMEN PILOTS OF WORLD WAR II

Aronova, Raisa E. *Nochnye ved'my* [Night Witches]. Moscow: Sovetskaia Rossiia, 1969.

Belyakov, Vladimir. "Russia's Women Top Guns." *Aviation History* (March 2000): 34–40.

Capin, M. Patricia. "Soviet 'Girls' Can't Fly: Common Sense." *Minerva: Quarterly Report on Women and the Military* 5, no. 4 (1987).

Cottam, Kazimera J. *Women in Air War: The Eastern Front of World War II*. Nepean, Canada: New Military Publishing, 1997.

———. *Women in War and Resistance: Selected Biographies of Soviet Women Soldiers*. Nepean, Canada: New Military Publishing, 1998.

———. *In the Sky Above the Front: A Collection of Memoirs of Soviet Air Women Participants in the Great Patriotic War*. Manhattan, Kansas: Sunflower University Press, 1984.

Dixon, Robyn. "Women of War: 'Night Witches' Recall Fighting Nazi Invaders With Suicidal Courage." *Los Angeles Times,* May 20, 2001, AA–4AA.

Duncan, Phyllis Anne. "How They Must Love Their Homeland." *FAA Aviation News,* May/June 2002, 20–25.

Erickson, John. "Night Witches, Snipers and Laundresses." *History Today* 40 (July 1990): 29–35.

Myles, Bruce. *Night Witches: The Untold Story of Soviet Women in Combat*. Chicago, Illinois: Academy Chicago Publishers, 1981.

The Night Witches: Soviet Air Women in World War II. Documentary film. Produced and directed by Sissi Hüetlin and Elizabeth McKay. London: Move A Mountain Productions, 1994.

Noggle, Anne. *A Dance with Death: Soviet Airwomen in World War II*. College Station, Texas: Texas A&M University Press, 1994.

Pennington, Reina. *Wings, Women and War: Soviet Airwomen in World War II Combat*. Lawrence, Kansas: University Press of Kansas, 2001.

———. "'Do Not Speak of the Services You Rendered': Women Veterans of Aviation in the Soviet Union." *Journal of Slavic Military Studies* 9, no. 1 (March 1996): 120–151; reprinted in *A Soldier and A Woman: Sexual Integration in the Military,* ed. Gerald J. DeGroot, and Corinna Peniston-Bird. London: Longman, 2000.

———. "The Propaganda Factor and Soviet Women Pilots in World War II." *Minerva: Quarterly Report on Women and the Military* 15, no. 2 (Summer 1997): 13–41.

Polunina, Ekaterina K. *Devchonki, podruzhki, letchitsy* [Girls, girlfriends, pilots]. Moscow: Izdatel'sky Dom "Vestnik Vozdushnogo Flota," 2004.

Rudneva, Yevgeniya Maksimova, and Irina V. Rakobolskaya, ed. *Poka stuchit serdtse: dnevnik I pis'ma geroia Sovetskogo Soiuza Evgenii Rudnevoi* [As Long as the Heart Beats: The Diary and Letters of the Hero of the Soviet Union Yevgeniya Rudneva]. Moscow: Izdatel'stvo Moskovskgo Universiteta, 1995.

Rybalkina, Natalia. "A Visit with the 'Night Witches,'" *Soviet Woman* (November 1990): 4–5.

Strebe, Amy Goodpaster. "Airwomen of the Red Star: World War II Soviet Women Combat Pilots." *Flight Journal,* 11, no. 2 (April 2006): 22–30.

———. "Marina Raskova and the Soviet Women Aviators of World War II." *Russian Life* 46, no. 1 (January/February 2002): 42–47.

Timofeeva-Egorova, Anna. "Derzhis' Sestrenka!" [Hold Fast, Sister!] *Voenno-Istoricheskii Zhurnal* (USSR) 3 (1983): 68–74.

WASPs and Witches: The History of Women Pilots Fighting for the Right to Fight. DVD. Documentary film. Produced and directed by Jamie Doran. Atlantic Celtic Films, 2000.

Zhenshchiny na za Shchite Otechestva 1941–1945 [Women in Defense of the Fatherland 1941–1945], vol. 3. Moscow: Russian Committee of Veterans of the War, 2000.

GENERAL WORKS ON WOMEN IN AVIATION/MILITARY/ SOCIETY/WAR—SOVIET UNION/RUSSIA AND GERMANY

Attwood, Lynne. "Rationality versus Romanticism: Representations of Women in the Stalinist Press." In *Gender in Russian History and Culture,* edited by Linda Edmondson, 158–176. New York: Palgrave, 2001.

Babichev, Sergei. "A Woman's Affair. (Russian Pilot Svetlana Protasova)." *Russian Life* 40, no. 3 (March 1997): 9–12.

Buckley, Mary. "Complex 'Realities' of 'New' Women of the 1930s: Assertive, Superior, Belittled and Beaten." In *Gender in Russian History and Culture,* edited by Linda Edmondson, 177–193. New York: Palgrave, 2001.

Campbell, D'Ann. "Women in Combat: The World War II Experience in the United States, Great Britain, Germany and the Soviet Union." *Journal of Military History* 57.2 (April 1993): 301–323.

CIA World Fact Book 2006, https://www.cia.gov/cia/publications/factbook/geos/rs.html#Military (accessed November 9, 2006).

Clements, Barbara Evans. "Later Developments: Trends in Soviet Women's History, 1930 to the Present." In *Russia's Women: Accommodation, Resistance, Transformation,* edited by Barbara Evans Clements, Barbara Alpern Engel, and Christine D. Worobec. Berkeley, California: University of California Press, 1991.

DiGuglielmo, Tina. "The Role of Women in the Soviet Armed Forces: Past, Present and Future." In *Beyond Glasnost: Soviet Reform and Security Issues,* edited by David Thomas Twining. Westport, Connecticut: Greenwood Publishing Group, 1992.

"Germany's 'queen of erotica' dies." *BBC News,* July 18, 2001. [Article online]. http://news.bbc.co.uk/2/hi/europe/1445272.stm (accessed September 27, 2006).

Griesse, Anne Eliot, and Margaret A. Harlow. "Soldiers of Happenstance: Women in Soviet Uniform." *Minerva: Quarterly Report on Women and the Military* 3, no. 3 (1985): 127–151.

Griesse, Anne Eliot, and Richard Stites. "Russia: Revolution and War." In *Female Soldiers—Combatants or Noncombatants?: Historical and Contemporary Perspectives,* edited by Nancy Loring Goldman. Westport, Connecticut: Greenwood Publishing Group, 1982.

Herspring, Dale R. "Women in the Russian Military: A Reluctant Marriage." *Minerva: Quarterly Report on Women and the Military* 15, no. 2 (Summer 1997): 42–59.

Hoffmann, David L. *Stalinist Values: The Cultural Norms of Soviet Modernity 1917–1941.* Ithaca, New York: Cornell University Press, 2003.

Jones, David E. *Women Warriors: A History.* Washington, D.C.: Brassey's, Inc., 1997.

Jones, Ellen. *Red Army and Society: Sociology of the Soviet Military.* Boston, Massachusetts: Allen & Unwin, 1985.

Julnes-Dehner, Noel. "Under Fire: Soviet Women Combat Veterans." *Minerva: Quarterly Report on Women and the Military* 15, no. 2 (Summer 1997): 1–12.

Kalinin, M.I. *On Communist Education: Selected Speeches and Articles.* Moscow: Foreign Languages Publishing House, 1953.

Karash, Yuri. "Training of a Female Cosmonaut." *Space.com,* January 26, 2001. (http://www.space.com/news/spaceagencies/woman_cosmonaut_010126.html) (accessed September 17, 2006).

Karpov, Vladimir. *Russia at War 1941–1945.* New York: The Vendome Press, 1987.

Keyssar, Helene, and Vladimir Pozner. *Remembering War: A U.S.–Soviet Dialogue.* New York: Oxford University Press, 1990.

Kirschenbaum, Lisa A. "Our City, Our Hearth, Our Families": Local Loyalties and Private Life in Soviet World War II Propaganda." *Slavic Review* 59, no. 4 (Winter 2000): 825–847.

Lapidus, Gail Warshofsky. *Women in Soviet Society: Equality, Development and Social Change.* Berkeley, California: University of California Press, 1978.

Mamonova, Tatyana. *Russian Women's Studies: Essays on Sexism in Soviet Culture.* New York: Pergamon Press, 1989.

Mathers, Jennifer G. "Women in the Russian Armed Forces: A Marriage of Conven-
    ience?" *Minerva: Quarterly Report on Women and the Military* 18, nos. 3–4
    (Fall/Winter 2000): 129–141.

———. "Women, Society and the Military: Women Soldiers in Post-Soviet Russia."
    In *Military and Society in Post-Soviet Russia,* edited by Stephen L. Webber,
    and Jennifer G. Mathers. Manchester: Manchester University Press, 2006.

Murmantseva, Vera Semenova. *Zhenshchiny v soldatskikh shineliakh* [*Women in
    Soldiers' Overcoats*]. Moscow: Voenizat, 1971.

Pushkareva, Natalia. *Women in Russian History from the Tenth to the Twentieth
    Century.* Armonk, New York: M.E. Sharpe, Inc., 1997.

Russian Women Aviators: A Panel Discussion, featuring Nadezhda Kuzhelnaya,
    Svetlana Protasova, and Lidiya Zaitseva. VHS. The Museum of Flight,
    Seattle, Washington, March 18, 2006.

Sakaida, Henry. *Heroines of the Soviet Union 1941–1945.* Oxford: Osprey Publish-
    ing Ltd., 2003.

Saywell, Shelley. *Women in War.* Markham, Ontario, Canada: Penguin Books Can-
    ada Ltd., 1985.

Smith, Gregory Malloy. "The Impact of World War II on Women, Family Life, and
    Mores in Moscow, 1941–1945." PhD diss., Stanford University, 1989.

Stalin, Joseph. *The Great Patriotic War of the Soviet Union.* New York:
    International Publishers, 1945.

Stites, Richard. *The Women's Liberation Movement in Russia: Feminism, Nihilism,
    and Bolshevism 1860–1930.* Princeton, New Jersey: Princeton University
    Press, 1990.

Stoff, Laurie. "They Fought for Russia: Female Soldiers of the First World War." In
    A Soldier and A Woman: Sexual Integration in the Military, edited by Gerard
    J. DeGroot, and Corinna Peniston-Bird. London: Longman, 2000.

Warren, Marcus. "MiG Pilot Flies in Face of Russian Male Prejudice." *Daily Tele-
    graph,* Issue 1504, July 8, 1999 [article online] http://www.telegraph.co.uk/
    htmlContent.jhtml?html=/archive/1999/07/08/wpil08.html (accessed Septem-
    ber 17, 2006).

INDEX

46th Guards Night Bomber Aviation Regiment, 2, 15, 18–19, 22, 25, 35, 44, 92 n.23;"Night Witches," 19, 49

73rd Guards Fighter Aviation Regiment, 26

122nd Aviation Group, 18, 23

125th Guards Dive Bomber Aviation Regiment, 2, 15, 18–19, 22, 43, 58, 72

586th Fighter Aviation Regiment, 2, 18, 22, 26–27, 88 n.14

587th Day Bomber Aviation Regiment. *See* 125th Guards Dive Bomber Aviation Regiment

588th Night Bomber Aviation Regiment. *See* 46th Guards Night Bomber Aviation Regiment

A-24 Douglas Dauntless, 54

Adams, Henry, 50

Aeroflot, 81

Air Corps. *See* U.S. Army Air Corps

Air Force. *See* U.S. Air Force

Air Transport Auxiliary (ATA), 3, 6, 43, 68

Air Transport Command (ATC), 7, 38, 60

Akimova, Alexandra, 47

Amosova-Taranenko, Serafima, 46, 56

Anderson, Nonie Horton, 11

André, Jacques, 44

Arlington National Cemetery, 79

Army Air Corps. *See* U.S. Army Air Corps

Army Air Forces. *See* U.S. Army Air Forces

Arnold, Henry H. "Hap," 6, 8, 12, 14, 62–66

Arnold, W. Bruce, 76–78

Aronova, Raisa E., 23

Atatürk, Kemal, 3

Avenger Field, Texas, 8–10, 39, 42, 52, 63, 66–67

Aviation: women in World War I, 30; women in after World War II, 67–69, 77

B-17 Flying Fortress, 11

B-26 Marauder, 32

B-29 Superfortress, 11–12

Belyakov, Vladimir, 27

Bendix Transcontinental Air Race, 5

Blank, Adaline, 9

Blitzkrieg, 5

Bochkareva, Mariya, 29–30

Bondareva, Anna, 22

Bondareva, Antonina Spitsina, 72

Borisoglebsk Aviation Training
   Center, 81
Bosca, Caro Bayley, 43
British Ferry Command, 3
Brok-Beltsova, Galina, 19, 25, 88 n.14
Brown, Marion Schorr, 40–41
Brown, Reginald, 79
Budanova, Ekaterina V. ("Katya"), 28,
   34
Bulechek, Annelle Henderson, 59
Bulgakova, Maya, 74
Burton, Harold, 62

Camp Davis, North Carolina, 39,
   53–54
Carl, Ann Baumgartner, 11, 33, 52
Carter, Jimmy, 12, 78
Chayes, Antonio, 78
Chechneva, Marina, 21
Chuikova, Ekaterina Petrovna, 70
Civil Aeronautics Administration
   (CAA), 5, 8, 38, 61, 63, 65
Civil Air Patrol, 77
Clements, Barbara Evans, 20
Clovis Army Air Field, New Mexico,
   11
Coast Guard. See U.S. Coast Guard
Cochran, Jacqueline: aviation records,
   5; background of, 4; breaks the
   sound barrier, 33, 75; at Camp
   Davis, 54; death of, 76; disbandment
   of the WASP, 66–67; femininity of,
   41; formation of the WASP, 1, 6–9,
   12, 14; meets General Henry "Hap"
   Arnold, 6; militarization of the
   WASP, 60–61, 63; relationship with
   Nancy Harkness Love, 7; reunion of
   the WASP, 76; and WAC, 60; after
   World War II, 75
Cole, Jean Hascall, 10, 33
Congress. See U.S. Congress
Costello, Bill. See House Resolution
   4219
Costello, John, 12, 62–63
Cottam, Kazimiera Jean, 16

Dahl, Roald, 11
Degtereva, Nadezhda, 30

Deryabina, Klavdia, 46
Deynekin, Pyotr, 80
DiGuglielmo, Tina, 79
Disney, Walt, 10, 67
Dolgorukaya, Princess Sophie
   Alexandrovna, 30

Earhart, Amelia, 5, 15, 33, 68–69
Eddy, Vivian Cadman, 68
Edwards, Rebecca, 31
Englund, Irene, 79
Englund, Julie, 79

Fedotova, Ekaterina, 24
Felker, Phyllis Tobias, 37
femininity, 30–31; of Soviet airwomen,
   48; of WASP, 41–42, 60, 65
Fenton, Isabel, 61
Fifinella (WASP mascot), 11, 29

Fifinella (official Avenger Field plane),
   67
Fillmore, Carole, 38–39
Fort, Cornelia, 31–32
Franco, Francisco, 5

Gardiner, Libby, 32
Gelman, Polina, 34, 55
gender issues, 2, 49–50, 58, 81–82;
   Soviet airwomen, 20, 22, 45, 47, 72;
   WASP, 37–38, 40–42, 60, 65
GI Bill of Rights, 66
Gilbert, Marge, 10
Gökçen, Sabiha, 3
Goldwater, Barry, 77
Gorbachev, Mikhail, 28
Gott, Kay, 3
Grachev, Pavel, 80
Granger, Byrd Howell, 38, 62
Grizodubova, Valentina, 16–17, 20, 35
Guruleva-Smirnova, Yevgeniya, 44

Harman, Jean Downey, 40, 51–52, 66,
   68, 79
Harmon Trophy, 5
Hartmann, Susan M., 13
Hero of the Soviet Union, 1, 15, 17,
   21, 23, 28, 44, 72

Herspring, Dale R., 29
Hill, Joseph, 62
Hitler, Adolf, 1, 3, 5
Hobby, Oveta Culp, 31, 60
Hodgson, Marion Stegeman, 7, 9, 32, 39, 57
Hoffmann, David L., 17
Honey, Maureen, 30
House Civil Service Committee, 64
House Resolution 3358, 62
House Resolution 4219, 62–63
House Veterans' Affairs Committee, 77
Howard Hughes Airport, Houston, Texas, 8
Hughes, Howard, 5

James, Teresa, 39
Jaros, Dean, 43
Jones, Caryl, 52
Jones, Ellen, 82
Junkers Ju-87, 3

Kalinin, Mikhail I., 71
Karasyova-Buzina, Nina, 45
Kaverin, Veniamin, 80
Kerensky, Alexander, 30
Khaldei, Yevgeny, 48
Kirilina, Anna I., 88 n.14
Kirschenbaum, Lisa A., 31
Knight, Clayton, 6
Kravchenko, Valentina, 25
Kuzhelnaya, Nadezhda, 81

Ladies Courageous, 43
Landry, Katherine, 40
Las Vegas Army Air Field, 52
Lavrinenko, Vladimir, 27
Lavrinenkov, Vladimir, 44
Lazarsky, Barbara Ward, 57
Lea, Luanne C., 42
Lee, Ah Ling ("Hazel"), 31
Lend-Lease Act, 6
Litvyak, Lidiya ("Lilya"), 18, 26–28, 34, 48
Lomako, Vera, 16
London, Barbara Erickson, 65, 68, 78, 82

Love, Nancy Harkness, 7–8, 76
Love, Robert H., 7, 76
Lovett, Robert A., 6
Luftwaffe, 3

Maier, Erwin, 27
Mamonova, Tatyana, 74
Maresyev, Alexei, 19
Marine Corps Women's Reserve (MCWR), 29
Markov, Valentin, 45
Mathers, Jennifer G., 73–74, 80
McClellan, Anne, 31
McConnell, Mary Elizabeth, 64
McCormick, Jill, 63
McCreery, Jean Terrell Moreo, 38
Meniailenko, G.N., 45
Merced Army Air Field, California, 67
Merryman, Molly, 65
Messerschmitt 109, 3, 28
MiG-29, 80, 85 n.3
Minton, Madge Rutherford, 61
Mishakova, Olga, 71
Moggridge, Jackie Sorour, 43
Moore, Jean, 66
Moorman, Dorothea "Didi" Johnson, 11
Morrison, James, 61, 63
Moses, Beverly, 52
Mussolini, Benito, 5

New Castle Army Air Field, Delaware, 63, 77
"New Soviet Woman," 20, 49, 57, 73
"Night Witches." See 46th Guards Night Bomber Aviation Regiment
Noggle, Anne: A Dance with Death, 44, 47, 56, 58, 81; as a WASP, 31, 51–52, 58, 68
Nosal, Dusia, 23

Odlum, Floyd, 4
Office of War Information (OWI), 30
Olds, Robert, 7
Operation Barbarossa, 1
Orr, Joanne Wallace, 40
Osipenko, Polina, 16–18, 20, 25, 35
Osoaviakhim, 21–22

P-47 Thunderbolt, 39, 63
P-51 Mustang, 11, 38–39, 54
Pe-2 dive bomber, 18, 43, 70
Po-2 biplane, 18–19, 49
PT-19 (Fairchild), 9
Pasportnikova, Inna V., 23, 34
patriotism, 1, 28, 31–34, 42
Pearl Harbor (attack on), 1, 3, 8, 29, 32, 66
Pennington, Reina, 17–18, 23, 33–34, 44, 49, 73
Pimenov, Yuri, 19
Polunina, Ekaterina K., 27–28, 88 n.14
Popova, Nadezhda, 19, 24, 26, 35, 46–48, 51, 55, 73
propaganda, 17–18, 30–31, 43–44, 49, 57
Protasova, Svetlana, 80–81, 85 n.3

Rakobolskaya, Irina, 26, 44, 49, 56, 73
Ramspeck Report, 63
Ramspeck, Robert, 62
Raskova, Marina: background of, 16; character of, 15, 17–18; daughter of, 23; death of, 25, 45; 1938 flight, 1, 16–17, 35; formation of aviation regiments, 15, 18, 22–23; popularity of, 17–18; relationship with Stalin, 18; as role model, 25; training of pilots, 24-25
Rawlinson, Mabel, 53
Reitsch, Hanna, 3
Riabova, Ekaterina, 25, 72
Richards, Faith Buchner, 65
Richey, Helen, 68
Roach, Eileen, 53–54
Rodina, 16–18, 35
Roosevelt, Eleanor, 4, 6
Roosevelt, Franklin D., 6, 66
Royal Air Force, 11
Rudneva, Yevgeniya ("Zhenya"), 57
Russian Air Force: women in, 80–82

Saywell, Shelley, 24, 48
Seip, Margaret, 52
Semper Paratus Always Ready

(SPARs). See U.S. Coast Guard
Senate Resolution 1810, 62
Senate Veterans' Affairs Committee, 77
Severson, Helen, 52
Shakhovskaya, Eugenie, 30
Sholokhova, Olga, 43
Shutsy-Reynolds, Florence, 10, 52, 67–68
Silver, Gertrude Tompkins, 54–55
Smirnova, Mariya, 47, 56, 72
Soviet Air Force, 18, 27, 44
Soviet Airwomen: after World War II, 71–73; awards and medals, 1, 16, 18, 23, 25, 28, 71–72; camaraderie of, 51, 55–57, 70; death of, 34, 55–57; demobilization of, 70–73; discrimination of, 2, 37, 43–45, 82; media coverage of, 49; motherhood and, 17, 20–21, 23, 31, 71–73; physical challenges, 2, 24, 44–46, 56–57, 72; stress of combat, 26, 45–47, 56–57; training of, 23–24; types of missions, 18–19, 22, 44, 46, 56; uniforms, 23
Stalin, Joseph, 15–18, 21, 44, 49, 70
Stalingrad, 23, 25, 27
Stege, Juliette Jenner, 9
Stimson, Henry, 61
Strizhi ("Swifts") aerobatic team, 80
Strother, Dora Dougherty, 11, 53, 77–78
Sweetwater, Texas, 8, 33, 60, 64, 66, 76

Tanner, Doris Brinker, 9, 14, 32
Taylor, Betty, 54
Terekhova, Klavdia, 72
Tibbets, Paul W., Jr., 11
Timofeeva-Egorova, Anna, 46, 91 n.36
Tupolev Tu-134, 81
Turner, Betty Stagg, 64

Uhse, Beate, 3
U.S. Air Force (USAF), 53, 68, 76–79
U.S. Army, 79
U.S. Army Air Corps, 6, 42; Ferry Command, 7

U.S. Army Air Forces (USAAF), 6–8, 12, 14, 37, 40, 53, 60, 62–63
U.S. Coast Guard, 29
U.S. Congress, 6, 12, 38, 43, 60–63, 65–66, 76–78
U.S. Marine Corps, 29
U.S. Navy, 29
U.S. War Department, 61–62, 65

Verges, Marianne, 76, 78
Veterans Administration, 78
Volkova, Valya, 44

Ward, Roy P., 67
Watson, Florene Miller, 42
White, Christine, 55–56
Williams, Betty Jane ("B.J."), 11, 40, 68
Women Accepted for Voluntary Emergency Service (WAVES), 29
Women Airforce Service Pilots (WASP), 1–2, 76; after World War II, 67–68, 72; awards and medals, 65, 78; creation of, 6, 8; death of, 1–2, 52–54; disbanding of, 14, 64, 67; friendships of, 51, 55–57, 70; male pilots' attitude toward, 37–42, 63–65, 82; media coverage of, 12, 14, 42, 49, 60–61, 65; militarization of, 12, 14, 43, 59–60, 63, 66, 77–78;

movie made about, 43; physical challenges, training, and requirements of, 2, 7, 9, 38, 40; as test pilots, 11–12; as tow-target pilots, 11, 53–54; training of, 8–10, 33; types of missions, 1, 8, 11, 38, 53–54, 66; and Soviet women veterans, 57–58; uniforms, 59–62; veteran status, 2, 12, 77–78; "zoot suit," 9
Women's Army Auxiliary Corps (WAAC), 29
Women's Army Corps (WAC), 29, 31, 60
Women's Auxiliary Ferrying Squadron (WAFS), 8, 31, 38, 42, 78
Women's Flying Training Detachment, (WFTD), 8
Woods, Ruth, 68
World War I: women in, 29–30
Wyall, Marty, 8, 59

Yak fighters, 16, 18, 27, 34
Yeager, Chuck, 33, 75
Yeltsin, Boris, 80
Yerokhina-Averjanova, Olga, 57

Zhigulenko, Yevgeniya, 15, 17, 35, 48
Zhitova-Yushina, Raisa, 45, 57

ABOUT THE AUTHOR

Amy Goodpaster Strebe is a journalist and historian. She is the author of *Desert Dogs: The Marines of Operation Iraqi Freedom* (2004). Strebe holds a master's degree in history from San Jose State University. She has written extensively on the U.S. armed forces and is one of the leading experts on the women military pilots of World War II.